CREATIVITY FOR MANAGERS

For my parents

CREATIVITY FOR MANAGERS

ALAN BARKER

THE INDUSTRIAL SOCIETY

First published in 1995 by
The Industrial Society
Robert Hyde House
48 Bryanston Square
London W1H 7LN
Telephone: 0171–262–2401

© The Industrial Society 1995

ISBN 1 85835 148 0

British Library Cataloguing-in-Publication Data.
A catalogue record for this book is available from the
British Library

Typeset by: The Midlands Book Typesetting Company Loughborough
Printed by: Lavenham Press
Cover design: Nicky Downes
Cartoons: Martin Shovel
The Industrial Society is a Registered Charity No. 290003

CONTENTS

introduction

For many people, creativity and management are polar opposites.

When I told the MD of a successful training organization that I was writing a book on creativity for managers, he replied: "They aren't interested in creativity. They want to know how to run their companies better."

Work — all work, from sweeping a floor to running a global corporation — is a creative activity. It is the means by which we transform the world and make something new. We can see the effect of sweeping a floor or making a product; the effects of management are not so obvious. A manager, by definition, *allows* others to work effectively.

> *Management is about human beings. Its task is to make people capable of joint performance.*
>
> [Peter Drucker]

Management is about 'making it happen'. Hence the continued emphasis on the *practical*, action-centred aspects of the job:

* integrating people in a common venture;
* gaining commitment to shared goals and values;
* helping people to learn;
* communicating;
* fostering responsibility;
* measuring performance;
* minimizing costs.

Yet *all* of these are essentially mental activities. Without effective thinking, we would be unable to perform a single one.

When you don't have enough information to tell you what to do, you have to think. When you have too much information to make an obvious decision, you have to think. When you are faced with several possible courses of action, you have to think.

> *You think when you want a result which is better than what would happen without it.*
>
> [Jerry Rhodes]

People tend to bring two broad styles of thinking to management, depending on whether they have been promoted on the basis of expertise or experience. Expertise involves thinking about specific areas of knowledge: technical or academic thinking, trained or educated to a high level. Experience allows a manager to apply knowledge about particular areas of work: pragmatic thinking about systems, procedures, or technology.

Both styles of thinking are relatively narrow. As managers, we have to think much more broadly, and often less rigorously. This shift from technical expertise or functional experience to less focussed thinking can be profoundly disorientating. Specialists must become generalists. Management, we learn, is about solving problems with inadequate information.

Creative thinking has, in the past, been linked directly to problem-solving. Unfortunately, it has also gained a reputation among managers as a 'fringe' activity: quite fun, but of little practical use outside the brainstorming session or training room. A friend of mine refers to it as 'basketweaving'.

We need to bring creative thinking out of the brainstorming session. We need to recognize and develop it as a core competency. This book will help you to make creativity part of your managerial toolkit.

Part One presents a simple model of thinking and suggests how you can develop the whole range of your mental activity.

Part Two introduces a set of techniques that will help you to find opportunities for creative thinking and make the most of them.

Part Three explores the skills we need to take creative thinking out into the organization: in promoting new ideas, in our conversations with colleagues and clients, and as part of coaching and teambuilding. Corporate culture is not a side issue when we are developing managerial creativity: it sets the bounds of possibility. We need to recognize where — and how — we can exert influence to make creativity welcome: not only as the means of stimulating innovation, but as a managerial style. These last chapters offer skills and techniques to help us to begin that task.

A number of people contributed to the writing of this book. I am grateful to Robin Davies, who set me thinking about creativity in management and, during the course of many conversations, kept me on the right track; to Chrissie Wright, who put her faith in an untried idea and supported it through the 'dark night of the innovator'; to Sheridan Maguire for his patience and good humour; and to my wife, Gill, who talked through so many of these ideas and inspired me with her own creativity.

PART ONE: PREPARING
FOR CREATIVITY

1 what is creativity?

We shall not cease from exploration
And the end of all our exploring
Will be to arrive where we started
And know the place for the first time. [T S Eliot]

What does the word 'creativity' suggest to you?

This is a question I ask at the beginning of my creative thinking courses. Usually, people's initial answers suggest that we think of creativity as something exceptional:

Being a genius
Making something out of nothing
Having a baby
Producing a work of art
Thinking of totally new ideas

Creativity is often seen as rare: some magical power that only a few people possess. When I say that I train creative thinking, one of the most frequent responses is: "That would be no good for me. I'm not a creative person."

We are all naturally creative. A day or two exposed to creative thinking can alert us to the vast reservoir of potential in our minds. At the end of my course, I ask people to review their definitions of creativity, and their answers suggest a wide range of connections with their own experience.

Being daring	*Escaping from stuckness*
Entertaining silly ideas	*Thinking in new ways*
Suspending judgement	*Unlearning*
Asking awkward questions	*Challenging assumptions*
Wishing for the moon	*Dreaming the impossible*
Making novel associations	*Making metaphors*
Changing your point of view	*Having a vision*
Solving problems in a special way	*Unblocking your unconscious*
Breaking old habits	*Releasing hidden energy*
Leaping in the dark	*Recovering your inner child*

Creativity is indeed magical: but it is a magic we can all use.

We need to escape from the idea that creativity is "something" you either have or lack. Like magic, or athletics, or management, creativity is a group of skills, aptitudes and techniques, organized for a particular purpose.

Joseph Campbell, the great mythographer, sees creativity as a journey.

> *Creativity consists in going out to find the thing that society hasn't found yet.*
>
> [Joseph Campbell]

"GOING OUT"

Creativity involves exploration: looking beyond the boundaries of our normal thinking and experience. To be creative, we must venture into areas we don't know well. This is why creativity is often described as "scary", "chaotic", "disorientating" and "elusive" — but also "thrilling" and "intriguing".

"TO FIND"

Creativity is a process of discovery: of uncovering, or bringing to light. Being creative is not so much about thinking as about *looking*.

"THE THING"

Creativity never makes something from nothing. What we find is already there. We simply hadn't noticed it before, or seen it that way, or recognised its potential.

"THAT SOCIETY HASN'T FOUND YET"

Creativity brings back from its searches something of benefit, that adds value to our lives or our work: a new product, a new service, a new theory or design, a hypothesis, an artwork, a new procedure, a relationship with another person.

Being creative, then, is a matter of going out, exploring, finding something new and bringing it back to be used.

THE CREATIVE JOURNEY

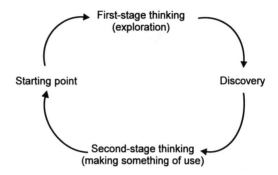

This two-stage creative journey — going out and returning — is a recurrent theme in this book. The first stage involves a mental excursion from a situation, in order to explore its potential. In the second stage, we return with a new idea and make some use of it.

2 thinking about thinking

Nothing is more dangerous than an idea when it's the only idea you have. [Emile Chartier]

Our well-being depends on good thinking. As life becomes more complicated, and the demands of work develop in ever more unexpected ways, thinking is the only skill that we can be sure will never become obsolete.

And yet we are not taught or trained to think. 'Thinking' as a subject is not on the National Curriculum. For this, and other reasons, a number of misconceptions have grown up around thinking, which need to be dispelled.

* **Thinking is not intelligence.** Thinking unintelligently may still achieve something. Intelligence without thinking is useless.

* **Thinking is not a function of education.** Highly educated people are not necessarily good thinkers; and many people with little education can think extremely effectively.

* **Thinking is not the accumulation of information.** An increase of knowledge is not thinking: it is simply hoarding. Too much information can seriously hamper our ability to think.

* **Thinking is not only the operation of logic.** It also involves looking, exploring, choosing, designing, evaluating and having hunches. It includes

7

considering priorities, objectives, alternatives, consequences and other people's opinions.

* **Thinking is not an alternative to doing.** We can certainly use thinking as an excuse not to act; and we can act without thinking. The reason we do both so much is that we regard thinking and action as opposed. They are not. Effective thinking improves the effectiveness of our actions; and our actions are a rich source of good ideas.

Perception and judgement

We can imagine thinking as a process in two stages.

First-stage thinking is concerned with perception: we *recognize* something because it fits into some pre-existing pattern. In first-stage thinking, we *encode* experience to make it easier to deal with. We *name* an object or event; we translate complex activity into an equation; we simplify a structure by drawing a diagram.

In **second-stage thinking,** we make judgements about the data by manipulating the code. Having named something as, say, a 'cup', we apply logic, language, custom and aesthetics to judge its effectiveness as a cup. Having labelled a downturn in sales as 'a marketing problem', we use market research, spreadsheets, past experience and critical scrutiny of the marketing department to judge how best to solve it.

> *Perception determines what we know; judgement decides what we know about what we know.*
> [Philip Goldberg]

We are very good at second-stage thinking. We are educated to manipulate language and mathematical symbols. We are encouraged to 'reason': to use logic, to analyse and categorize, to argue, debate and construct watertight channels of cause and effect. We are taught, too, to evaluate: to use critical thinking to decide whether something is good or bad, moral or immoral, 'correct' or 'incorrect'.

Our second-stage thinking is highly sophisticated. We can even build computers to do it for us. Indeed, for most of us, 'thinking' *is* second stage thinking: "the first stage is taken for granted," says Edward de Bono, "and often assumed not to be there at all."

We are not nearly so skilled at first-stage thinking. We have virtually no techniques or tools to help us stop and examine our perceptions.

Yet no computer will never give a good answer if the input is incorrect: "rubbish in, rubbish out", as any programmer will tell us. And no amount of sound second-stage thinking will produce a good answer if our thinking at the first stage is faulty.

> *We are beginning to realize that most of the trouble with our thinking results from our inability to do anything about this first stage.*
> [Edward de Bono]

If we decide that the cup is not a cup but a trophy — or a vase, a mug, a chalice — our second-stage thinking about it will change. Our 'marketing problem' may actually be a 'product quality problem', a 'distribution problem', 'a personnel problem', a 'macroeconomic problem' — or a subtle combination of all five.

THE RISKS OF 'LEAPING TO JUDGEMENT'

A little boy chases a ball into a busy road. His behaviour, in business terms, is admirably goal-oriented: his objective is well-focussed and he is pursuing it with great efficiency. Yet, by forgetting to stop, look and listen, he has placed himself in grave danger.

We, and our organizations, are all too often just like this hapless child. We formulate a strategy and clarify our objectives; we identify tactics and milestones; we allocate resources and make budget projections. By keeping our eye on the ball, however, we fail to look around: to ask whether our environment is 'safe', or whether the ball is worth pursuing.

Such 'leaping to judgement' — closely focussing on second-stage thinking *at the expense of first-stage thinking* — can put us at great risk. Like the child, we need to:

STOP! LOOK! LISTEN!

THE RISKS OF 'LEAPING TO JUDGEMENT':
some examples in management

New product development	*Emphasis on engineering the product rather than seeking alternative ways of achieving the same effect*
Introducing new IT systems	*Automating existing processes rather than reorganizing the processes to take advantage of IT-based opportunities*
Contractual negotiations	*Addressing pre-conceived 'issues' rather than*

---

	questioning the assumptions on both sides of what the issues might be
Responding to customer complaints	Perceiving the complaint as 'something to be dealt with' rather than as a wider opportunity to improve the product or service
Reducing quality failures	Working too hard to 'weed out' defective products rather than tracing errors back to their source and 'building quality in'
Corporate strategy	'Re-engineering' organizational structures rather than spending time asking: "What business are we in?"

The tools and techniques of creative thinking help us to stop, look and listen: to sharpen our powers of perception and exercise a little first-stage thinking.

Jung's four psychological functions

The great Swiss psychologist, Carl Jung, developed this two-stage model of mental process into two sets of paired complementary functions: **sensation and** intuition; **feeling** and **thinking.** Jungians understand sensation and intuition as functions of perception, and feeling and thinking as functions of judgement.

Jung's model indicates that there are two ways in which we perceive: through our senses, and by means of intuition. Intuition helps us to see the reality that lies *beyond* what our senses tell us: the deeper meanings, relationships and patterns. "Intuition," says Jung, is "perception of the possibilities inherent in a situation."

JUNG'S PSYCHOLOGICAL FUNCTIONS

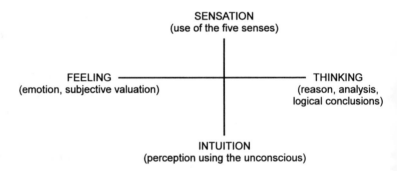

SENSATION
(use of the five senses)

FEELING
(emotion, subjective valuation)

THINKING
(reason, analysis,
logical conclusions)

INTUITION
(perception using the unconscious)

Sensation *(ie, sense perception) tells you that something exists;* thinking *tells you what it is;* feeling *tells you whether it is agreeable or not; and* intuition *tells you whence it comes and where it is going.*

[C G Jung]

If we want to become more skilled in first-stage thinking, Jung's model suggests two courses of action:

* sharpen our senses;

* develop our intuition.

Sharpening our senses is not essentially difficult, though seeing or hearing clearly may be hampered by emotion, conflict, fatigue or sheer noise. Developing our intuitive skills, on the other hand, is not so easy.

Yet, without doubt, we use our intuition all the time: whenever we make a choice or a decision; every time we speak to somebody; in every meeting and interview; whenever we examine a set of figures or a project plan. And, as with any other mental faculty, we can use it well or poorly.

The problem, of course, is that intuition uses the unconscious: we realize something without understanding *how* we come to know it. We cannot summon up an intuition deliberately. We can, however, do something to prepare for it, to recognize our intuitive insights when we catch them, and to help intuition to contribute more effectively to our thinking.

A lot of confusion can arise around the word 'intuition'. To help to make sense of it, let me make clear my own interpretation of the word.

*   Intuition is a function of *perception*. It can help us to see a situation more fully. It is not a function of *judgement*: it cannot, by itself, tell us how to act.

*   An intuition may come to use in disguise. We must be ready to interpret the *form* of our insight and, if necessary, revise it.

*   Intuition is not a substitute for thinking. It is a part of thinking. We must be ready to submit an intuitive insight to rigorous second-stage evaluation.

3 developing your intuition

Be one of those on whom nothing is wasted.

[Henry James]

Intuition is "perception of the possibilities inherent in a situation".

In Jung's view, intuition uses the unconscious to tell us, not that something exists, but "whence it comes and where it is going". In any situation, intuition will suggest:

* how it may have come about;

* how it may develop;

* what implications it may have for other situations;

* how we might respond to it;

* what new ideas it might provoke in our minds.

Like other visitors from the unconscious (dreams, for example, or flashes of humour), intuitions have paradoxical qualities. They are unexpected, yet they 'fit'; they are personal, yet feel as if they have come to us from outside; they may lack detail, yet be very strong.

Our responses to intuitions, too, may be contradictory. We feel closely involved in them, yet oddly objective about them; we may have a strong emotional reaction to them, yet feel a calm, cool certainty that they are true; we are absorbed by them, yet detached from them.

Recognizing intuitions

Recognizing these paradoxical qualities will help us to know when intuition is speaking to us. It is like a shy person trying to be heard at a party. With so much noise, so many distractions, and so many other calls on our attention, the 'still small voice' of intuition is often drowned out.

Even if we hear it, we may not listen. If we are not accustomed to taking notice of intuitive insights, if they seemed to let us down in the past, we may distrust them. If our organization is driven by the values of judgement — measurement, rationality, systematic procedures and finding 'the right answer' — we may not be encouraged to use our intuition as a thinking tool.

*   **When do intuitions come to you?**

When you are closely involved in the matter? Shortly after taking a break from it? While engaged in some other activity?

*   **What is your general state of mind when they arrive?**

Relaxed, at rest, even sleepy? Distracted? Concentrated?

*   **At what time of day do you seem to be most intuitive?**

On waking? Late at night?

*   **Are you more intuitive about some things than others?**

About technical problems or dealing with people? Making decisions or sizing up a situation?

*   **Are there any activities that seem to be conducive to intuition?**

Cooking? Washing up? Gardening? Playing or listening to music? Walking? Swimming? Meditation? Daydreaming?

* **Have you ever tried to be intuitive?**

What did you do? Did it work?

* **Are your intuitions sudden, or gradual?**

Do you need time to ponder? Do you trust your immediate reaction?

INTUITION GAMES

* *Make a log of all the moments when you might have been using intuition during one day. Which were the most significant? How might you act on your insights?*

* *When was the last occasion when intuition would have been helpful but it didn't happen? What was in the way?*

* *Allow your intuition to make minor decisions for you: deciding what to wear for an appointment; ordering at a restaurant; buying a small gift for a friend.*

* *Make predictions about everyday events: who is on the phone when it rings; who will win a sports fixture; tomorrow morning's newspaper headline; a colleague's first words when you meet tomorrow; this week's sales figures. Betting is not recommended!*

* *Turn the sound down during a TV soap or sitcom and work out what the story is. You may need a friend to watch with you, wearing headphones, to verify your description; alternatively, tape the section you are watching and play it back.*

It is easy to allow an intuition to pass, even to acknowledge it, and yet not register its worth. Reflect on any intuitions that may come to you.

* **What is the basic message?**

An insight (that something is true)? An instruction (to do something or avoid doing it)?

* **In what form did it come to you?**

Verbally? Visually? Physically (a 'gut feeling')?

* **How strong was it?**

Vivid? Vague? Sudden? Prolonged? Has it been repeated? If so, has any part of it changed?

* **How does the intuition make you feel?**

Exhilarated? Relieved? Depressed? Warm? Certain?

* **What do you think about it?**

How logical is it, in hindsight? How reasonable? How appropriate?

* **How surprising is it?**

How unlike custom or the dictates of authority?

* **What is your overall reaction to it?**

Are you inclined to accept or reject it?

Testing your insight

Having made this last decision — whether to accept or reject your insight — submit it to ruthless internal cross-examination. Remember: your intuition may have come to you in disguise!

TESTING YOUR INSIGHT

If you are inclined to accept, ask:

* *Is it intuition or emotion?*

* *Is it merely wish-fulfilment?*

* *Am I simply acting on impulse?*

* *Do I just want to bolster my image as an intuitive person?*

* *Am I being mentally lazy?*

* *Is it rebelliousness?*

* *Am I frightened of uncertainty?*

If you are inclined to reject, ask:

* *Is it because I'm labelling it as something else: silliness, paranoia, whimsy, emotion?*

* *Is is something I'd rather not know?*

* *Am I afraid of criticism?*

* *Am I frightened of mockery?*

* *Am I merely yielding to external authority or other people's views?*

* *Am I being self-critical?*

* *Am I afraid of the new?*

* *Am I being too demanding?*

* *Am I selling myself short?*

* *Am I frightened of taking a risk?*

If your intuition survives this onslaught of hard questions, submit it to some rigorous second-stage thinking.

* **Defend your insight logically**

A good insight can be defended rationally, even if the process of having it is irrational.

* **Look at it from all sides**

List its positive features, its negative features, and its interesting features, in that order.

* **Work through the implications and consequences of the intuition**

What else would be true if this were true? Does the intuition explain other evidence?

Who would be affected if you acted on it? How? When? How might they respond?

* **Find a way to test your intuition as safely as possible**

Conduct an experiment or some gentle research. Try something out.

* **Talk about it to somebody else**

This may be one of the best ways of exposing the intuition to the light of day. We become clearer about the true content of an intuitive insight when we explain it to others; and a fresh pair of eyes can provide a new perspective.

Remember that articulating or defining an intuition may distort it or lessen it in some way. What we gain in clarity we may pay for in loss of depth.

Every theoretical explanation is a reduction of intuition. [Peter Høeg]

What inhibits intuition?

Research into managers' use of intuition has made one particularly significant finding: people rarely feel comfortable admitting openly that they have used intuition to make managerial decisions.

The most powerful factor inhibiting your use of intuition may be the corporate culture you operate in. If an organisation is internally competitive or strongly conformist, you will probably not find much encouragement to exercise your intuition. If colleagues or senior managers demand 'hard' justifications for every decision, you may find yourself compelled to dress up your intuitive insights in 'data clothes': exhaustive cost-benefit analyses, resource management plans and market research.

* **How does your organization respond to intuitive ideas?**

Organizations can foster an aggressive attitude to problem-solving. For every problem there must be a single, perfect solution; making decisions quickly is seen as a sign of strength, and delay is interpreted as weakness.

The response may be different at different levels of the organization. Decisions at the highest level are often made on the basis of very narrow, second-stage thinking.

* **How do your colleagues react to intuitive ideas?**

How would they respond if you became more intuitive in:

— deciding what to wear at work;

— altering the agenda of a regular team meeting;

— discussing new product ideas;

— organizing the daily schedule;

— predicting future market or political developments?

If they show resistance to using intuition, ask why. Is there pressure from higher up, or from the market, or from tightly controlled systems? What might you do to counter such resistance, or avoid it? How might you make the use of intuition more acceptable in your team, or among your colleagues?

Opening the door

We cannot command intuition to work for us; like Aladdin's genie, it may initially appear by accident. We can, though, make ourselves available for it to visit.

* **Recognize inhibiting factors in yourself:**

low self-esteem, an excessive need for security, fear of change, an intolerance of uncertainty, an urge to keep control, dishonesty.

* **Recognize external inhibitors:**

lack of time, lack of extensive background knowledge, other people's feelings/desires/opinions/arguments, intermediate targets, resistance in the wider culture of the organization.

* **Learn how to recognize stress:**

loss of clarity, 'treadmill thinking', lack of concentration, milk frustration. Take a break!

* **Seek quite times.**

Try to build them in to your timetable.

* **Balance mental stress with physical stress.**

Take up a regular physical activity; try yoga; go for a brisk walk.

* **Practise flexibility in your thinking.**

Look for the ambiguities, the vague or awkward information. Seek new perspectives on what you're doing;

examine your emotional or physical responses to ideas or events.

* **Expose yourself to a wider range of experience.**

Do something, read something, go somewhere — different.

* **Lighten up.**
Try not to take matters too seriously. Humour is one of the great indicators that intuition is at work.

* **Relax the process of decision-making.**

Build in a stage when intuitive ideas can be expressed openly. Demand a pause before coming to important decisions.

* **Focus on ends, not means.**

Clarify your goals. Try to imagine unique, perfect solutions to problems. Ask: "what's the *real* problem?" Recognize when you are becoming obsessed with processes and targets.

With practice, we can become more familiar with our intuitions. They are unlikely to appear if we are stressed, or if we feel our colleagues are likely to dismiss them. They are more likely to appear when the circumstances are relaxed, co-operative and open. As managers, we may even be able to encourage others to offer their own intuitions: to indicate by our own example that we value intuition as a part of the decision-making process.

> *If we issue an open invitation and make intuition feel that visits are welcomed at any time, it can become a perfect guest, showing up on all the right occasions, dressed properly and bearing felicitous gifts.*
>
> [Philip Goldberg].

4 creativity and intuition

Creativity is the ability to see relationship where none exist.
[Thomas Disch]

What have been the most important learning experiences of your life?

They were probably single, overwhelmingly powerful events: falling in love; the birth of a child; a sudden bereavement; a chance encounter; an accident. We may have sought them, in a spirit of adventure; or they may have thrust themselves on us, unbidden or unwelcome. We have certainly been surprised by them.

These experiences have a quantum effect: they result in sudden shifts in *perception*. They show us something familiar in a strange, new light, or bring disparate elements of experience into an unexpected synthesis. "It made me see things differently," we say; "the scales dropped from my eyes"; "I saw the light"; "I see things differently now." And, like quantum events, they are usually accompanied by a release of energy: an explosion of laughter (or tears).

This sort of learning is unlikely to take place in a conventional educational or training situation. It is non-incremental: it doesn't happen in steps, by working through a book or a course of lessons. It is a *discontinuity* in our experience.

Such discontinuity is at the heart of creative thinking.

The four stages of creativity

Graham Wallas, in 1926, identified four stages in the creative process.

* Preparation

* Incubation

* Illumination

* Verification

Preparation involves worrying at a problem, investigating it 'in all directions'. This hard work seems to be essential, if only to exhaust the mind to such an extent that intuition is allowed to take over.

Incubation is the conscious mind 'letting go' of the problem. We 'sleep' on it: forget about it, do something else, take a break, perhaps literally go to sleep. The material goes 'underground', where intuition sets to work.

Illumination occurs when elements of the problem 'click' into a new pattern — what Wallas calls a 'happy idea'. It is the discontinuity, the 'quantum leap' that radically alters our perception of a situation.

Illumination is well named: it is as if a light is suddenly switched on, and we are able to see what was previously invisible. We are 'enlightened'.

Verification involves checking that the 'happy idea' makes sense: applying logic and evaluation to justify and validate it.

ARCHIMEDES AND THE CROWN OF GOLD

Archimedes of Syracuse was the most celebrated mathematician and inventor of his time — the second century BC.

One day, his patron, Hiero, tyrant of Syracuse, was offered an ornate crown. He suspected that the goldsmiths were attempting to trick him by adulterating the gold with silver. He asked Archimedes' opinion.

Archimedes knew the specific weight of gold — its weight per unit volume. If he could find the crown's volume, he would need only to weight it to establish its purity. But how was he to measure the volume of such an irregularly-shaped object? He could not melt it down, or beat it into a rectangular block . . .

He thought long and hard, reviewing all his knowledge of geometry, worrying at the problem and returning again and again, increasingly frustrated, to his starting point.

Finally, he gave up and went to the public baths to relax.

Now Archimedes took baths regularly, and had no doubt noticed many times how the water level rose as he got in. On this occasion, however, he suddenly realized that this simple fact was the solution to his problem. His body displaced its own volume of water, which could simply be measured by the pint. He had, in effect, melted down his body! He could do the same with Hiero's crown.

His elation at this discovery was such that he leapt from the tub and capered out onto the streets of Syracuse stark naked, shouting: "Eureka!" — meaning "I have found it!"

BISOCIATION

Archimedes' 'happy idea' is the result of juxtaposing two seemingly unrelated elements: the problem of measuring the volume of an irregularly shaped object; and taking a bath.

Arthur Koestler has named this kind of event 'bisociation'. A pun is a simple example of bisociation: it depends for its effect on seeing two unrelated meanings in one word. Riddles, jokes, crossword clues, brain teasers: all use bisociation.

Creative ideas, too, are often the result of juxtaposing elements that are normally unconnected. And, like jokes or riddles, they often provoke laughter: the laughter of delighted, astonished recognition. The mind has a unique and apparently limitless ability to make connections between ideas. The more distant the ideas from one another, the more creative the connection.

What is intriguing about these creative connections is that they are perfectly logical — with hindsight. *Making* them, though, involves no logic at all. It is a matter of first-stage thinking: of **seeing** the connection, rather than working it out.

TAKING A BREAK

Can we deliberately incubate? Bisociation is an intuitive process, and, as we have seen, we cannot summon an intuition at will. And yet, we can do a lot to help intuition to do its work.

The difficulty is that we tend to think too hard. Our minds run along the paths of habitual thought, making tried and tested connections. We refuse to let them relax sufficiently for them to make new connections.

Good ideas rarely come 'out of the blue'. Sitting around waiting for inspiration will not work. Insight is always founded on hard work and a concentration on the matter in hand. You cannot relax unless you have first exerted yourself.

> *Fortune favours the prepared mind.*
> [Louis Pasteur]

There are three broad strategies for bisociation available to us.

* Escaping from stuckness

* Looking for the bigger picture

* Choosing a creative approach

The approach we take will depend on the nature of the task, our own favoured style of thinking, and external circumstances.

Escaping from stuckness

This strategy is useful when our thinking seizes up. The mind starts 'tramlining', goes round in circles, or simply stops working. We run out of ideas and find it impossible to see anything but obstacles in our path.

'Stuckness' usually occurs because our thinking is too focussed. Archimedes knew precisely what he had to do, but it seemed impossible. We may know the goal of our thinking — to write an awkward letter, to summarize a set of figures for a Board meeting, to improve the quality of a service to a quantifiable level, to reduce the unit cost of a product — but the *means* elude us.

We need to cultivate a sense of when best to take a break: before the warning signals of 'stuckness' get too strong. Watch for:

*   'treadmill thinking';

*   mild frustration;

*   fatigue;

*   loss of concentration;

*   signs of irritability;

*   physical or mental stress.

Of course, we might use this strategy as an excuse for simply 'giving up when the going gets tough'. In fact, a far greater danger is that we will work too long before taking a break. Pressure to deliver, disgust at our own 'stupidity', guilt — not to mention the 'work ethic' with which we may punish ourselves for 'not doing anything' — push us beyond the limit of effective hard work, into stressful drudgery.

We are using bisociation here to *escape* from stuckness: to find some new connections that will move us forward.

* Look up from the problem. Gaze out of the window.

* Stand back from the problem. Literally. Walk to the other side of the room.

* Take a break: go to the coffee machine, the washroom or the canteen.

* Engage in physical exercise. Talk a walk for a few minutes.

* Work on some other, easier aspect of the problem. Distract your mind with routine.

* Go somewhere different: another department; an art gallery; a park. Look for echoes of the problem in some element of the unfamiliar environment.

Useful questions to escape from 'stuckness' include:

* "What is my *real* goal here?"

* "Where is the sticking point? Can I turn that into a goal?"

* "Suppose I simply ignore the obstacle? Remove it? Pretend it doesn't exist?"

* "What do I really want?"

* "Why am I getting tense?"

* "What's annoying me about this?"

* "How could I look at this differently?"

Looking for a bigger picture

This strategy is useful when our thinking refuses to take shape. The mind, far from being stuck, is racing: juggling ideas furiously, piling fact on fact. We can't 'switch off'.

The problem here is a *lack of focus*. We are overwhelmed with information: by its complexity or its sheer volume. We know so much about the issue that we cannot begin to make use of it. Perhaps the demands being made of us are vague or contradictory. Writing a report or proposal; making a policy or strategic decision; explaining the economic implications of a technical problem; selecting a new team member from a large number of candidates — in every case we are hampered by *too many ideas*.

We might decide to defer the decision for as long as possible: to immerse ourselves in information, exploring, discovering, refusing to focus on a clear course of action until intuition tells us to stop. The time to take a break will be when we:

* become obsessed with details or side-issues;

* lose sight of the larger picture;

* find ourselves wanting to leap to a decision;

* cannot explain the situation clearly;

* still have time before the deadline for action.

Of course, such a strategy might leave us open to the charge of indecisiveness. And indeed, we could probably go on amassing information for ever! The real danger, however, is that we will make the decision too quickly: complete the report too swiftly; commit resources without proper thought of the long-term consequences; argue too simplistically; promote or hire somebody on a whim. Such 'premature closure' is common in many business decisions.

We are using bisociation here to *synthesize* material: to find the connections hidden in the information that will make sense of it as a whole.

*   Write down the goal of your thinking.

*   Establish essential criteria for success.

*   Explain the situation to a colleague.

*   Do something else! Leave the problem alone for a while.

*   Later, try to recall the matter without using your notes. What comes to mind first?

*   Draw a diagram of the problem.

Questions to ask:

*   "Why am I looking at this material?"

*   "How am I going to *use* this information?"

*   "What does all this add up to?"

*   "Can I represent this information graphically?"

*   "Am I trying to do too much at once?"

*   "What do I really want?"

*   "Why am I confused?"

Choosing a creative approach

Escaping from stuckness and looking for the bigger picture are useful interventions in everyday thinking. We might decide, however, on a more thoroughgoing creative approach: to take a longer excursion from the problem with the hope of bringing something radically different back.

Such a creative detour is unlikely to happen by itself. We must *make the choice* to take it.

Most managerial work is located in a cycle of routine, procedures, rules and known solutions. Many problems can be solved within this cycle; indeed, our solutions help to reinforce the very routines and procedures by which we found them.

Traditional problem-solving proceeds in three stages:

1. Identify the problem.

2. Identify the cause.

3. Remove the cause.

And, along the way, we will ask questions such as:

*   Have we tackled a similar problem in the past?

*   Might we tackle this problem in the same way?
*   What makes this problem similar — or different?

*   Can we pick a specific example of the problem and work it out?

*   Can we divide the problem into parts and solve each part?

However, not every problem can be solved like this. Indeed, some problems can't be solved at all! Creativity will help us to solve problems when:

*   they have no single identifiable cause;

*   we cannot remove the cause(s);

*   we have inadequate information, or too much!

*   the information is ambiguous;

*   we have little or no precedent to follow;

*   the variables are difficult to measure;

*   the information doesn't clearly indicate what to do;

*   time is limited;

*   we want to do something different.

In such cases, we can decide to move from the cycle of routine to the creative cycle: to leave the old routines and habits of thinking behind for a while and explore new possibilities.

It can be a difficult decision to make. We are entering uncharted territory; we may not find anything new; we are rejecting what has always worked for us in the past; what we find may have consequences far beyond the original problem.

The consequences of *not* making this choice, though, might be worse. Suppose we commit resources to a project that answers the wrong question? Suppose we do things the way we've always done them, only to discover after the event that we might have cut costs dramatically with a little creative thought? Suppose one of our

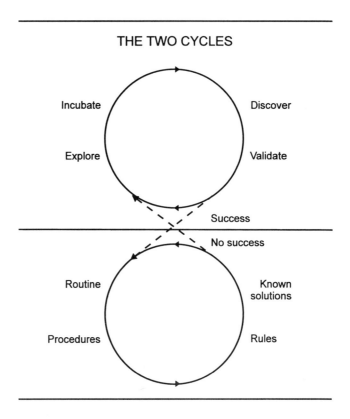

THE TWO CYCLES

Incubate

Discover

Explore

Validate

Success

No success

Routine

Known solutions

Procedures

Rules

competitors were to choose the creative option and discover something that destroyed our advantage?

> *And the trouble is, if you don't risk anything, you risk even more.*
>
> [Erica Jong]

The two stages of creative thinking

Creative thinking is a journey into the unknown. It is an excursion, a trip away from current reality, to find the potential hidden within it and something new that we can bring back.

THE TWO STAGES OF CREATIVE THINKING

First stage	Second stage
soft divergent	hard convergent

'Find something new'	'Get something done'
What if?	Will it work?
Why not?	Can we do it?
What associations can we find?	Has it been tried before?
What rules can we break?	Does it fit in?
What assumptions are at work?	Have we got the resources?
What is this like?	Is the timing right?
What analogy could we use?	Who can help?
What metaphor suggests itself?	How much will it cost?
Suppose the problem were a solution?	Suppose it fails?

The **first stage** involves moving away from a problem or situation in order to explore and investigate its potential. We widen our perceptions by questioning assumptions, by looking at material in new ways or by making random juxtapositions with unrelated ideas. This is *diffuse thinking, divergent thinking* or *radiant thinking*. Our purpose is to *find something new.*

The **second stage** judges the new ideas we have found and brings them back into the world as something of use. We evaluate and judge them, using *convergent*, or *focussed thinking*: logic, categorization, measurement and analysis, comparison against objectives. Our purpose is to *get something done.*

We will need to be well-equipped for such an exciting journey. In Part Two of this book, we will examine and exercise useful tools and techniques to take with us.

PART TWO: ELEMENTS OF CREATIVITY

5 finding problems

Problems cannot be solved by thinking within the framework in which the problems were created.

[Albert Einstein]

Creativity is less about solving problems than about finding them.

What could be more absurd? Why spend time looking for problems? Aren't there enough already?

Well: sometimes, part of the problem is the way we are looking at it; and part of our task is to reformulate the problem itself.

What is a problem?

Faced with such a question, most people would probably suggest these answers:

* Something that must be solved (removed/minimized/ignored)

* Something that cannot be solved (removed etc . . .)

* Something we are set

* An obstacle

* Something that causes pain or stress

* Something we'd rather not have

Thinking further, they might add:

* Something that *can* be solved

* Something we set ourselves

* A challenge

* Something that gives us the opportunity to do better

* A catalyst

We seem to have two broad definitions of problems. What are the differences between them?

PRESENTED PROBLEMS AND CONSTRUCTED PROBLEMS

Presented problems are those which come to us, or are given to us, or happen to us.

> *Problems are presented to us by the outside world.*
>
> [J R Hayes]

Examples would include:

* a piece of machinery breaking down

* a target set us by somebody else

* being stuck in a traffic jam

* a sudden shift in interest rates

The defining feature of a presented problem is a *discernible gap* between initial conditions and 'goal conditions'. We know that something is wrong; we know what is wrong; we will know when it has been put right; and we may or may not know, more or less, how to put it right.

Constructed problems, by contrast, are problems that we make for ourselves. There may not be anything specifically wrong; but we are interested in the possibility of improvement, or change, or doing something different. Examples would include:

*   gaining a qualification

*   improving our performance

*   innovating a new product

*   increasing market share

*   improving an existing procedure or service

*   working out a long-term strategy

> *A problem is a chance for you to do your best.*
> [Duke Ellington]

The defining feature of a constructed problem is the *created gap* between current conditions and a potential future. There may not even have been a problem until we constructed it. We literally 'make a problem for ourselves'.

Presented problems arise out of a tension between what is and what ought to be. Constructed problems include a tension between what is and what might be.

We experience the first kind of tension as **emotional tension.** It is like the tension between two jammed machine parts: a stress that threatens to cause damage. It is unwelcome, unpleasant and exhausting. It can be relieved in only two ways: by applying pressure; or by separation. We can seek to overcome the problem, or avoid it: fight or flight.

We experience the second kind of tension as **creative tension.** It is like the tension in a taut rubber band, stretched between current reality and our vision of the future. It is potential energy: it is exciting and energizing, and provokes movement.

> *People don't resist change. They resist being changed.*
>
> [quoted by Peter Senge]

'How to'

The first step in tackling a problem creatively is to transform it into a constructed problem.

The easiest way to do this is to cast it as a 'how to' statement.

* a piece of machinery breaking down:
  how to repair the machinery

* a target set by somebody else:
  how to meet the target

'How to' immediately suggests possible courses of action: "I might . . ." We have taken ownership of the problem and converted it into a task, a challenge, an opportunity.

We are now in a position to explore the potential of the constructed problem. Each 'how to' itself suggests new 'how to's':

* being stuck in a traffic jam:

  how to get out of the jam
  how to stop becoming enraged
  how to use the time productively
  how to reorganize my schedule

* a sudden shift in interest rates:

  how to counter the effects of new interest rates on our trading
  how to use the new interest rates to our advantage
  how to make our products more competitive abroad
  how to improve our profile abroad

> *how to make ourselves less vulnerable to shifts in rates*
>
> *how to improve our position in the domestic market*

It is this range of 'how to's' that is important. The problem as presented was difficult to solve. By transforming it into a constructed problem, we are able to stand back from it, explore it, play with it and find new potential within it.

TASK DESCRIPTION

Use this checklist to generate as many 'how to' statements as possible from your initial constructed problem.

How to . . . .

Background
How has the task come about? Why does it need to be done? What is the context?

Ownership
Do you truly 'own' the task? Why are you involved? Where does it 'hurt' (emotional/creative tension)? How does it affect you personally? What is motivating you to find a solution? What does it feel like (look, sound, taste, smell, touch)?

Past efforts
What's already been tried or considered? By whom? Do any solutions already exist? Why are they unsatisfactory?

Power to act
What are you in a position to do? What resources are at your disposal? What authority do you have? What are you willing to do?

What constraints are you operating within? Who else is involved? How?

Ideal solution

A big wish. If miracles could happen, what would you ask for? What is your vision for the future? Describe a world in which this wish has come true. Wish for the impossible!

Backwards planning

This is a useful technique for clarifying goals. By regarding the initial 'How to' as a solution rather than a problem, we move backwards, asking what higher-level problem it might solve. We can repeat the process with the new problem, and so on.

Higher-level 'how to's' will be more general than the original; they will also bring our personal aspirations into clearer focus.

BACKWARDS PLANNING

Take your initial 'How to' statement and ask:

* *"If I achieve it, what will that give me?"*

* *"And if I had that, what would it give me?"*

Try to focus at each level on benefits to you, *rather than anybody else. Ask:*

* *"If I had that, would I want it?"*

* *"Might there be any other way of achieving it?"*

Example

> *"How to increase business with existing key accounts by 10% over the next quarter."*

* *"If I achieve it, what will that give me?"*

> *More business! Actually, more solid business, more stable relationships.*

> * *"And if I had that, what would it give me?"*
>
> *More time to develop the relationships: less time chasing business.*
>
> * *"And if I had that, what would it give me?"*
>
> *Greater power to plan.*
>
> * *"And if I had that, what would it give me?"*
>
> *The opportunity to improve what I do.*
>
> *Our range of constructed problems now includes:*
>
> *How to increase business with existing key accounts by 10% over the next quarter.*
>
> *How to build more stable relationships with my key customers.*
>
> *How to find the time to develop relationships with key customers.*
>
> *How to spend less time chasing new business.*
>
> *How to be able to plan more effectively.*
>
> *How to improve what I do.*

Finding the way forward

Before long, you will be faced with an array of 'how to' statements. You will need to choose which to pursue.

You might divide the list roughly into three categories.

*   **Realistic courses of action** that you could take immediately. They may be known solutions you had forgotten about. You might consider applying them now, or putting them to one side as fallback solutions.

* **Embryonic ideas** needing modification or development. Useful as starting points for later exploration if necessary.

* **Implausible ideas.** They are vague, nonsensical or Incomprehensible. These are the ideas with the most creative potential.

Pick a 'how to' that appeals to you: it makes you laugh or feel good. Maybe it makes you say: "Wow! If we could do that, all our problems would be solved."

Armed with a new, exciting description of our task — probably something a long way from our original thought — we are ready to move into the next stage of the creative process, where we look for opportunities to create bisociations and generate ideas for solutions.

6 mental gymnastics

Keep your hat on. We may end up miles from here.

[Kurt Vonnegut]

We think by organizing experience into patterns. Information, the result of this process, is an expression of the *shape* of our thinking.

The mind is *self-organizing*. Throughout our lives, there is a continuous and subtle interplay between the patterns of our thinking and our experience. Every new experience will change our mental patterns in some way; and those patterns themselves determine how we interpret experience. Experience and mental patterns *together* organize themselves into information.

Patterns are extremely useful to us because we can *recognize* them, *repeat* them and *plan* with them.

> *Note down examples of patterns you have already used today:*
>
> *SEQUENCES*
> *CYCLES*
> *PROCESSES*
> *SIMILARITIES*
> *PROBABILITIES*
> *MAPS*
>
> *Have you missed any?*

As a simple example of our reliance on mental patterns, consider the number of pieces of clothing you

49

are currently wearing. How many possible ways are there of putting them on?

A simple calculation will provide a surprising answer. We can (theoretically) put on seven pieces of clothing in 5,040 possible sequences (7 x 6 x 5 x 4 x 3 x 2). For ten pieces of clothing, the number is 3,628,800! Of course, not every one of these sequences is realistic: we cannot put on our shoes before our socks, or trousers before underwear. Practicality reduces this figure to a few thousand.

Without a clear pattern to govern this simple operation, we would still be working out how to get dressed at bedtime.

Mindsets

Our mental patterns grow by extension, over time. Those we use the most (or value highly) will become the strongest; those we use rarely (or value least) will tend to fade.

The danger, of course, is that a strong mental pattern will *dictate* what you look for, what you see, how you interpret it and what you do about it. Such a mental pattern has become a *mindset*. If a new piece of information fails to fit the mindset, we would rather reject the information as irrelevant — or wrong — than challenge the mindset itself.

We may even fail to notice critically important information. A mindset will *select* the information it needs.

> *Stop reading and look around you for FOUR items containing the colour yellow. Do it now. See how easy it is to find what you're looking for?*

Mindsets are useful for dealing efficiently with repeated situations. They become dangerous "when," as Tudor Rickards puts it, "things have changed but everything looks the same."

Creativity involves breaking mindsets: challenging the accepted patterns by which we interpret experience, cutting across mental patterns in order to find new connections, or making new patterns that *more usefully reflect reality*. And, because mindsets operate below the level of consciousness, we need to 'trick' the mind into thinking differently.

All the tools and techniques in this chapter are designed to help you engage in mental gymnastics: to leap from old ideas to new ones, to turn ideas on their heads, and to find 'mental muscles' you never thought you possessed! Like any other form of exercise, the benefits of these tools will grow with repeated use.

ASSOCIATIVE THINKING

Every word we use has patterns of meanings associated with it. The patterns will vary from person to person: 'green' to one person might suggest a mass of environmental issues; to another, it will suggest their relative inexperience in a new job; to a third, the light that signals a clear road ahead.

> *Put the word 'road' in the middle of a piece of flip chart. Round it, in a circle, write down all the words you associate with it. Write the first words that come to mind; take no more than one minute.*
>
> *It can be useful to do this exercise with a colleague. Do not discuss your associations as you note them.*
>
> *Now compare the results. How many words do you have in common? Probably not many!*

This simple exercise helps us to access associative patterns that we would normally ignore. It helps us to break mindsets and can act as a springboard for richly creative ideas.

It is the *diversity* of new ideas that is so valuable. Every person's pattern of associations is unique. It is possible to generate a large number of novel associations very quickly; each association is the beginning of a new train of thought.

> *The human brain can make infinite number of associations; and our creative thinking potential is similarly infinite.*
>
> *[Tony Buzan]*

PATTERN DIAGRAMS

Pattern diagrams use associative thinking to help us see the overall shape of a piece of mental territory. By emphasizing the *links* between ideas in a field, they encourage us to think more freely *and* display the shape of our thinking simultaneously.

To make a pattern diagram:

* Take a plain piece of paper: as large as possible and in landscape format (long side horizontal).

* Put a *visual image* of the idea you are considering in the middle.

* Write down anything that comes to mind in association with that word or image.

Write *single* words, in BLOCK CAPITALS, along lines radiating from the central word or image.

Single words have more free 'hooks' to associate with than groups of words; block capitals will help the diagram to be more easily read; and the structure of your thinking will be much clearer if all the lines on the map are pointing *outwards* from the centre.

* Every line must connect to another line

* Look for *themes* — words expressing bigger ideas which will tend to be placed nearer the centre of the diagram; and *details*, which will connect to themes as twigs to branches and expand the idea across the diagram.

* Look for words which connect to the senses: seeing, hearing, touch, taste and smell. Look, too, for words to do with movement.

* Use *colour*, *images* and *symbols* throughout the diagram: to highlight structure, stimulate your imagination and bring your pattern diagram to life.

* Give each branch a boundary line which 'hugs' the branch and gives it a unique shape.

* Keep going! Your brain is able to generate ideas far more quickly than you can write; but only if you leave it as free as possible to do the job. If a word occurs to you, do not analyse it; note it down and look for the connections it triggers. Order and structure will take care of themselves. If your pencil stops moving, you are thinking too hard.

Pattern diagrams score over conventional note-taking (in lists) because:

* links between ideas are more obvious — and less rigid;

* reading the diagram encourages us to rethink and revise our thoughts;

* new information can be added more easily and neatly;

* every diagram is different, more personal and immediate — and therefore less vulnerable to mindsets;

* the diagram encourages the generation of ever more ideas.

They are useful in any situation where information must be generated, gathered, structured or recalled:

* preparing a report
* drafting a letter
* revising for an exam
* planning a presentation
* organizing the agenda for a meeting
* taking notes from a meeting, conversation, presentation or lecture
* planning a schedule

They will help you to break free of mindsets, see new connections and generate ideas. Pattern diagrams help you to see and develop the shape of your thinking.

HIDDEN PERSUADERS

Hidden persuaders are the rules that govern our behaviour without our being aware of them.

Where are the rules in your organization? Most of us would make a list which includes:

* procedures;
* structures;
* systems;
* regulations.

Perhaps, after a moment's thought, we might add:

* habits;
* conventions;
* culture ('the way we do things round here').

> *Creative thinking may mean simply the realization that there is no particular virtue in doing things the way they have always been done.*
>
> [Rudolf Flesch]

We are encouraged from earliest infancy to follow rules. This is often for good, practical reasons. "Don't touch the oven"; "don't cross the road without looking"; "don't steal" — all make a lot of sense if we want to survive in society.

Rules are useful. They help things to run well. Organizations need systems, procedures and structures to make sure that the stationery cupboard is full and that the toilets flush.

We tend, though, to forget their most important characteristic. Rules are temporary. They are in constant need of revision. This idea is worrying. Change the rules and we no longer know where we are. We prefer to follow the rule even when it has outlived its usefulness.

Most of the rules we follow, of course, aren't documented. The way we dress (or the order in which we get dressed!), the route we take to work, the way we behave in the office, our attitude to our customers: all these are governed by 'hidden persuaders'.

---

* *Write down the five activities you most dislike in your job: in customer relations, administration, internal communication, whatever.*
* *Write down the reason for each one.*
* *Does that reason still exist? If not — why are you still doing what you hate doing?*

RULE REVERSAL

One of the best ways to challenge a rule is simply to turn it upside down.

Proverbs embody rules which are so hidden that they become 'common sense'. Reversing the proverb exposes the hidden persuader and challenges it.

* **Patience is a virtue.**

No it's not! Patience wastes time. We may wait so long that it never happens. Patience might mean that the other person is unaware that we want something from them. If we expressed *our impatience*, at least they'd get the message.

* **If at first you don't succeed, try again.**

Nonsense. If at first you don't succeed, *ask why*! Then try something different.

* **Too many cooks spoil the broth.**

Well: maybe they could each bring a unique ingredient to the broth. Maybe we need *even more* cooks. And who says it should be broth?

> *Look around your organization and find the mottos that it lives by. Try turning them upside down!*

DISCOVERING ASSUMPTIONS

Mindsets, too, are hidden persuaders. They provide the assumptions on which we base our thinking.

> *No matter how far one goes back in one's thinking, the starting point is always based on a set of assumptions. If one were not to use assumptions, one would never be able to think at all.*
>
> [Edward de Bono]

Assumptions, of course, like mindsets, operate unconsciously. In order to challenge them, we must first find a way of bringing them to the surface.

Pattern diagrams can help us to find assumptions. Take the following 'how to' statement:

"How to become more committed to Quality in everything we do."

To find some of the assumptions behind this statement, we can draw a pattern diagram round one of the words in it. We could choose any word in the statement; the most useful for our purpose is the most evocative, image-forming and in some way 'loaded'.

This pattern diagram is the result of five minutes' work. It identifies six patterns of meaning associated with the word 'committed'. Each of these patterns can be translated into new, suggestive and provocative 'how to' statements.

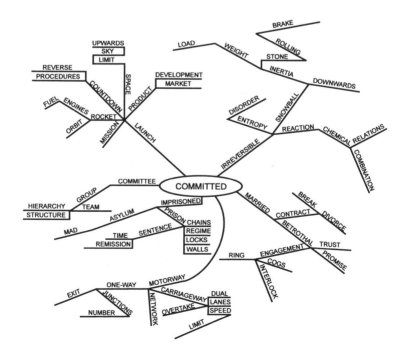

Married

Who are our partners? Customers? Suppliers? Service companies? Are we contractually bound — or only 'engaged'? Would a 'divorce' here or there be a good thing?

Marriage is about making promises. What promises do we make? Do we keep them? Do we *believe* in keeping them?

Marriage is also associated with the idea of families. How much is our company governed by 'family rules'? Who are the 'parents' and 'children'? Are there 'friends of the family' (associates, mentors, gurus, consultants)? How do we treat them?

How to break off our engagements.
How to keep our promises.
How to keep everything in the family.

Imprisoned

Are we imprisoned by our procedures or assumptions — or our mission? What are the chains that bind us and prevent us from seeking new products, new markets, new working relationships? How long is the 'sentence'?

How to break the chains that bind us.
How to reduce the 'sentence' of our imprisonment.
How to find new markets.

Motorway

How much like a motorway is our strategic thinking? Are we forcing ourselves to travel in only one direction? How many 'junctions' are we missing in our headlong drive down the 'fast line'?

Of course, motorways have a speed limit and all sorts of other regulations. Is our mission actually slowing us down? Are we prohibiting unnecessarily the use of certain 'vehicles' (procedures, smaller production units, less 'hi-tech' solutions)? What is our attitude to 'learner drivers'?

How to change direction.
How to break the speed limit.
How to train learners 'off the road'.

Committee

A committee is a group of people appointed to deal with some specific matter. The word relates to the original meaning of 'commit': to entrust.

How committee-bound are we? How do we make decisions? How do our working structures reflect our mission statement? How well do people work together in our organization? How much is entrusted to individuals or teams?

How to trust people more.
How to improve our decision-making.
How to delegate more effectively.

Take-off

Once a rocket fires its engines, it's committed to take-off. How often are we 'firing new rockets' (new products or services)? How effective are our 'countdown procedures' (how quickly do we develop the new product?) Do we have enough 'fuel' to launch our new products or services (people, resources, marketing?) — or to escape from the 'gravity' of past practices?

How to take off more safely.
How to develop products more quickly.
How to fuel the launch of a new product.

Irreversible

Commitment means no going back. Some chemical reactions cannot be reversed: once the compound is formed, the constituents cannot be separated out.

Are we committing our organization to irreversible changes? Are they what we want? Is the strategy going to snowball and be unstoppable — or impossible to steer?

How to create an irreversible reaction.
How to form a strong compound.
How to keep the snowball rolling.

DISCOVERING ASSUMPTIONS

Draw a pattern diagram around the word 'Team'. Encourage the rest of your team to do the same, individually.

Compare your results. What does the comparison suggest about the hidden persuaders that govern your attitudes to teamworking?

INTERMEDIATE IMPOSSIBLES

A development of rule reversal, intermediate impossibles are ideas that deliberately use impossibility or outrageousness to provoke new ideas.

To create an intermediate impossible, simply take the problem and find some way to reverse one of its elements. The result should be as impossible as possible! Our task is then to see how this outrageous idea can stimulate other, more realistic solutions.

A SIMPLE INTERMEDIATE IMPOSSIBLE

* *Take a few moments to write down all the possible uses of a brick.*

  "You can use a brick as . . ."
  "You can use a brick to . . ."
  "You can use a brick for . . ."

* *Throw all these ideas away.*

> * *Now write down as many possible non-uses of a brick as you can.*
>
>   *"You can't use a brick as . . ."*
>   *"You can't use a brick to . . ."*
>   *"You can't use a brick for . . ."*
>
> * *Take each non-use and transform it into a legitimate use.*
> * *A few examples:*
>
>   *"You can't use a brick for swimming."*
>   *(Polystyrene bricks?)*
>   *"You can't use a brick to wash with." (Brick of soap?)*
>   *"You can't use a brick for companionship."*
>   *("You're a brick!")*
>
> *Solutions will probably involve* **concept challenge***: our most basic assumptions about bricks are surfaced and blown apart.*

Use intermediate impossibles on one of your chosen "how to" statements.

How to reduce staff use of the telephone.

* "Electrify the telephone so that it administers a shock every time it's used."

* "Broadcast every call throughout the office."

* "Impregnate the handset with an offensive odour: the more you use it, the worse you smell."

and so on. Each outrageous idea might contain the seeds of a new, realistic approach.

Metaphorical thinking

What have the following in common?
An industry watchdog

A busman's holiday
The University of Life
A hive of activity
The ship of state
A ribbon development
A cast-iron guarantee

They are all metaphors. A metaphor describes something in terms of something else. Metaphorical thinking is perhaps the most intriguing variety of bisociation.

An analogy says that something is *like* another; a metaphor claims that it actually *is* the other.

We make metaphors constantly. We talk about *chain* reactions and political *footballs*; about the *heart* of the countryside or the *depths* of despair. We say that ideas are *fruitful*; that we have not been put *in the picture*; or that a project is soon to be *up and running*.

We learn through the use of metaphor: by relating what we don't know to what we already understand. Our ability to make and understand metaphors is proof of our innate creative potential.

> *The metaphor is probably the most fertile power possessed by man.* [Ortega y Gasset]

Organizations, professions and academic disciplines develop their own bodies of metaphor, which reflect the way they think.

Meteorologists, for example, use a lot of adversarial images to explain the weather; areas of high pressure *dominate* a system; the temperature *struggles* to reach the monthly average; cloud *builds up* and storms *break out*.

Economics, intriguingly, uses metaphors derived from water. Money *flows* or is *pumped* into the system; it is *deposited* in *banks*. Currencies rise and fall or *find their own level* against one another. Companies are *floated* on the Stock Exchange or have their assets *frozen*.

* Look for the metaphors at work in your own organization: in its literature, in the words people use in discussion. What do they tell you about the culture of the organization?

* Listen for metaphors at your next team meeting. Draw the team's attention to them. Do they fit a pattern? Extend the metaphors to trigger new ideas. Metaphorical thinking is at the very heart of creativity. By describing a problem in terms of something initially unrelated to it, we *transform* it into something else and allow ourselves to make connections that have not previously existed.

THE ANALOGY GAME

Suppose you are thinking about one of these:

* *life*
* *your job*
* *the way your team works*
* *your organization*
* *a current problem*
* *an idea you are developing*

Now make an analogy with one of the activities below by saying:

"This is like that because . . ."

Baking a cake	*Running a relay race*
Making love	*Changing a nappy*
Conducting a military campaign	*Mowing the grass*
Driving along a motorway	*Going on holiday*
Swimming the Channel	*Playing jazz*

Changing a lightbulb	*Looking for fossils*
Fixing the car	*Cleaning the windows*
Painting a picture	*Steering an oil tanker*
Flying to the Moon	*Training a dog*
Treating an illness	*Climbing Mont Blanc*
Acting on stage	*Playing roulette*

Try to develop the analogy. What elements are involved? How might they apply to the original situation?

One connection should lead to another. Let associations spark new ideas in your mind. You needn't make logical sense: puns, jokes, figures of speech are all useful in linking ideas.

*If you can't see how the two sides of the analogy relate, don't be tempted to give up. Persist, keep looking. There **is** a connection: your task is to find it! The extraordinary thing about making analogies is that anything can be linked to anything else —*
— with enough thought. The most useful analogy may be the least obvious one.

Virtual worlds

Several of the 'how to' statements generated earlier (from the word 'committed') are metaphorical.

How to keep everything in the family
How to break the chains that bind us
How to break the speed limit
How to take off more safely

— and so on.

Each of these could be the germ of a 'virtual world' around the metaphor. What would it be like to try to keep things in a family? How do you escape from a chain gang? What would it take to break the speed limit? What procedures would we use to launch a space rocket safely?

Explore the world you have created. Travel around in it. Examine your feelings as you enter it. Consider the consequences of actions you take in it.

Eventually, you can bring back your metaphorical discoveries and see how they might apply — metaphorically — to the original situation.

VIRTUAL WORLDS

Construct a list of possible worlds to use as sites for future metaphorical excursions. The following is only a brief list of suggestions.

* ***The natural world:***

  — animal societies; plants; plate tectonics; evolutionary cycles

* ***Other cultures and civilizations:***

  — archaeology; science fiction; tribal customs; history; mythology

* ***Other industries:***

  — aeronautics; mining; medicine; finance; agriculture; transportation

---

* **The sciences:**

  — physics; geology; astronomy; oceanography; philosophy; electronics

* **The arts:**

  — theatre; cinema; dance; music; painting; literature; sculpture

* **Sport:**

  — football; motor racing; marathon running; rally driving; fishing

* **The military:**

  — warfare; strategy; espionage

Consulting the oracle

Oracles are tools for bisociating. Like riddles or horoscopes, they are designed to help us to shift our perception.

We use oracles to introduce a random element into our thinking. We may shuffle and turn up cards (the Tarot); look at the patterns of tea leaves in a cup; open a book at random; or throw dice. Using the ancient Chinese oracle, the I Ching, involves tossing yarrow stalks (or coins) and performing a simple calculation to decide which part of the oracle to read.

Look where you least expect to find it.

[Philip K Dick]

The random element forces us out of our habitual ways of thinking. If we are to make use of it, we must *make* a connection; the analogy or metaphor that makes sense of the bisociation and gives us a new idea.

A DO-IT-YOURSELF ORACLE

You can use a dictionary as an oracle. Make sure it's a good, large one.

Take one of your 'how to' statements.

Now, pick four numbers at random. You could generate them on a computer; throw dice; draw cards from a pack; take numbers from the telephone directory; ask people for the number of the house they live in; or simply use the first four numbers you see as you look up from your desk!

The first three numbers give you the page of the dictionary to turn to; the last, the position of the word on that page.

The best words for this purpose are verbs or concrete nouns. If the word you pick is something else, use the first verb or concrete noun immediately following (or preceding).

How does this randomly generated word make sense in the context of the problem you are thinking about?

Suppose we are considering:

How to encourage my team to be more creative.

I generate four numbers at random:

3184

On page 318 of my dictionary I look for the 4th word.

Clack

(I used a very big dictionary!)

This is a sudden dry sound — as of two pieces of wood hitting together. We want ideas to clack together — like billiard balls. How could we create a game of mental snooker?

A clack may be unexpected and make us jump. Perhaps the element of surprise is important. Suppose we had a clacking machine in the office: two large pieces of wood that make a satisfying noise. Whenever one of us is stuck with a problem, they clack the machine as a signal that they want immediate random associations with a key word. (Perhaps they simply shout "Clack"!) Thirty seconds of brainstorming should provide enough ideas to get them moving. It could become a standard team procedure.

*The idea is a good one. It is **novel** (any other teams that use "Clack!" as a catchphrase?); **attractive** (it will instantly pull the team together for a few moments; it offers support; it's quick, high-energy, fun); and **feasible** (no complicated equipment involved; no need for planning or timetabling; no cost implications).*

Why don't we suggest it at the next team meeting?

7 evaluating new ideas

Every new idea is born drowning. [Andrew Bailey]

Innovators live in the real world. Creativity is not merely a matter of having new ideas; it also involves *implementing* them: turning the ideas into products, services or procedures that add value to an organization.

> *The weird ideas of a psychotic person may rank high in originality and novelty, but we would hardly regard them as creative. To justify the use of the term 'creative thinking' a thought product also has to satisfy the criterion of having some use or value.*
>
> [Geir Kaufmann]

Every idea has some merit. By looking at a proposed solution to a problem in depth, we bring ourselves closer to a clear definition of it.

The easiest way to do this is to examine the **positive, negative** and **interesting** aspects of our idea, in order. The discipline of attending to each set of features in turn will help us to think about the idea more objectively.

Looking for what is good about it will strengthen it, and give it credibility when it comes to be presented to others (who will be all too ready to criticize or reject it). Looking for its weak features will give us the opportunity to work on them, develop or eliminate them before they see the light of day. By assessing what is interesting about an idea, we begin to reveal its potential impact, and can begin to think about the challenges of implementing it.

*   Identify **positive** aspects of the idea: whatever makes it attractive. Don't worry if you can't think of many. Persist: think *only* about positive features. For each one, ask: "What further benefits would that bring?" For every benefit, ask: "How else could we achieve that?" Yet more new ideas may suddenly begin to emerge.

*   Now list the aspects that are **negative** or problematic: weaknesses, shortcomings, risks and dangers. For each one, ask: "So what is it I need to find?" — and try to answer with a 'how to' statement. In this way, a single presented problem can easily turn into half a dozen potential ways of improving the idea.

*   Finally, list the **interesting** aspects of the idea: implications arising from it, the consequences of implementing it, how it will affect other people, potential by-products or spinoffs.

At the end of this process you should have a solution that is:

*N*ovel
*A*ttractive
*F*easible

*   **Novel**

    Has it been tried before?
    Has it been put into practice anywhere else (by other teams; by the competition; in similar organizations)?

    Is it radically new or only new*ish*?

*   **Attractive**

    Do we like the idea?

Is it likely to be attractive to the organization?
Will it solve the problems that the organization considers most significant?
What are the specific benefits (cut costs; streamline operations; provide new markets; take us into a new product sector; improve our image with our customers)?
How will it fit our strategy, vision, culture or style?

* **Feasible**

Is there any flaw or inherent inconsistency in the idea? Could it work? Could we imagine it happening here, in this organization?

We might score our idea according to these criteria, and invite others to do the same. The idea's *NAF* rating will give some idea of whether it is worth developing and promoting further.

It will be rare that an idea will score highly on all three counts. A very new idea may be attractive, but assessing its feasibility may be difficult. A highly feasible idea is unlikely to be particularly new: it may even have been tried before.

A CHECKLIST FOR EVALUATING IDEAS

* *Is the idea simple? Does it seem obvious? Is it too clever, ingenious, or complicated?*

* *Is the idea exciting? Does it 'explode' in people's minds? Does it provoke cries of: "Why didn't I think of that?" If it doesn't quite explode, could you simplify it?*

* *Is it compatible with human nature? Could anyone accept it as reasonable?*

* *Is it direct and uncomplicated?*
* *Can you write a simple, clear and concise statement of it?*

---

* *Can it be understood by anybody working in the field?*

* *Is it timely? Would it have been better six months ago? What's the point of pursuing it now? Will it be better six months hence? Can you afford to wait?*

PART THREE: CREATIVITY
AND OTHER
PEOPLE

8 promoting new ideas

Who the hell wants to hear actors talk?.

[Harry M Warner, 1927]

Promoting an idea, as any advertising executive will testify, is a creative process in itself. Many of the tough problems that delegates bring to creative thinking courses are of just this kind:

> *How to sell an idea to my manager.*
> *How to gain the team's commitment to a new procedure.*
> *How to convince the Board to allocate funds for the project.*
> *How to win regional offices' approval for a new distribution system.*
> *How to interest an awkward client in a new product.*

There are two main reasons why implementation is so difficult.

* **Ego attachment ('I am my idea')**

This is the moment when we must sacrifice our attachment to our idea: to let it go out into the world and fend for itself. Like any anxious parent, we find it difficult to relinquish ownership of ideas that we have nurtured from birth. But we must.

* **Other people**

Making an idea work involves influencing other people. We will want them to do something different. We will have to convince them, not merely that ours is a good idea, but that it can work — and that, with their help, it *will* work. And experience suggests that people will be ready with lots of reasons not to be convinced.

---

20 IDEA KILLERS

It'll never work.
It's a bit too radical for this company.
We tried it before and it failed.
Hm. Now supposing we just changed this little bit, and that piece . . .

What's the point?

It's not relevant to our current strategic plan.
It'll cost too much.
We don't have the resources/staff/money/time/ expertise/room/systems . . .
You haven't thought it through.

That reminds me . . .

Not practical.
Too complicated.
It'll never catch on.
Of course, that's just the sort of idea we might expect from you.

Let's wait a bit.

I like the idea, but my manager . . .
You'll never get people to change.
That's not the way we do things round here.
What about the intangibles?

Good idea. We'll appoint a committee to look into it.

'Making it happen' has always won approval in organizations. People with good ideas may never be noticed; those who make things happen can expect to catch people's attention and be promoted. Management, after all, is getting things done with and through other people.

Locating a sphere of influence

To implement an idea in an organization requires three things.

*   Authority
*   Control of a budget
*   Ability

Wherever all three exist together, a *sphere of influence* develops. Unless an idea is implemented through a sphere of influence, it will not survive. This brutal fact cannot be ignored by any innovator: if we want to implement a new idea, we *must* have access to the spheres of influence.

They may not be where we think they are! In tightly structured, hierarchical organizations, the centres of power are few in number and easy to identify (though even here, we may be aware of 'the power behind the throne'). In flatter organizations, all three elements of executive power are — at least in theory — spread between teams, partnerships, business groups and autonomous units. Identifying and evaluating spheres of influence becomes more complicated. Implementing a new idea involves as much liaison and networking as it does influence and command.

You will need to find the sphere of influence that is relevant to your idea. It may not be a conventional centre of power.

* Who is making all the important decisions these days?
* What issues or concerns are driving the organization at the moment?
* What parts of the organization address those concerns most directly?
* How relevant is our idea to those concerns?
* In what directions do we want influence to move in the organization?
* What kind of authority would give our idea credibility (financial/technical/marketing/personal)?

Finding a sponsor

Some innovators take total control of the implementation process.

A novelist on a recent Booker Prize shortlist published the book herself after being turned down by a number of publishers. The inventor of Monopoly famously started by manufacturing the game in his garage.

If our idea is to grow, however, we will probably need a sponsor: somebody who can support the idea through their organizational or personal influence.

Finding the right sponsor is an important and tricky matter. Begin by asking:

* "Who owns the problem?"
* "Who owns the solution?"

The problem owner will certainly have an interest in sponsoring our solution. But we will also want to win over the future owner of the solution.

* Who would control the budget for implementing this idea?
* Who has access to the people and resources we will need?
* What is the nature of their authority in the organization?
* Are they likely to stay in the organization long enough to see our idea through?
* What is their past record on implementing ideas?

The most powerful sponsor will be the person who can do most to help us to implement the solution. We will recognize them, not only by their position in the organization (and the size of their budget!), but also by their innate authority and ability: their capacity to influence others, their status, the value others place on their expertise — and their past record as people who 'make things happen'.

SELLING THE SOLUTION

Having chosen our sponsor, we will have to find ways of persuading them to support our idea. To do this, we need to exercise *empathy*, projecting ourselves *into* their mind.

* How do they see the organization, and their place in it?
* What are their goals — immediate and long term?
* How can our idea help to achieve those goals?
* What are their needs — and how can our idea address them?
* What are their prevailing mindsets?
* What are their systems of values?
* What style of management do they operate?

We must present our idea *in their terms*, locating it in their network of priorities and plans. We must use their language. This does not mean being dishonest or 'economical with the truth'; it means imagining how the idea would look from their point of view.

> *It is pointless to suppose that if a solution is correct then there is no need to sell it — that its truth will shine for all to see. No one is obliged to accept anything he disagrees with.*
>
> [Edward de Bono]

Arguing the case for an idea is not a good way of selling it. Give somebody logical reasons for doing something and they will immediately start to find arguments for not doing it! Logic relies on adversarial thinking: on assembling propositions and counter-propositions in order to discover the truth. Our task as innovators is not to arrive at truth, but to *persuade somebody* to do something — and logic is probably the least efficient way to do it.

What, then, will convince your sponsor? The evidence of their senses.

In advertising jargon: 'the eye buys'. If at all possible, *demonstrate* your idea. Build a prototype or a model; create a worked example; apply your idea to a real situation and show the benefits. Better still, ask your sponsor to 'do it themselves'.

If a practical demonstration is not possible, do the next best thing: create an evocative *image* in your sponsor's mind, which will make an immediate, lasting impression and stimulate their imagination.

Search for ways of bringing the idea alive, of personalizing it, of making it concrete. Search for:

* examples from experience
* anecdotes

* analogies
* metaphors
* symbols

Do not rely on selling your idea on paper. Memos, reports and proposal documents are useful for supporting your idea with detailed evidence; by themselves, they are unlikely to be persuasive. Find a way to *talk* about the idea, either informally in conversation, or in a more formal presentation.

> *You'll never convince anybody by logic alone.*
> [Rudolph Flesch]

A presentation gives you an excellent opportunity to prepare your proposal and control how you sell it. But beware! It is also an opportunity for you to destroy it by overkill: to go into a wealth of unnecessary detail and confuse your audience.

Keep your message simple. Your task is to *inspire*: to create a shared vision of a future. You will do this most effectively by planting images in your audience's mind that will stimulate their imagination. You could create a set of fancy slides or overhead projections; but the most powerful images are those that you conjure up in your audience's mind.

PROMOTING AN IDEA: A CHECKLIST

* *Think about implementation as early as possible.*

* *Clarify your goal. Ask yourself: "What do I want to do? What's stopping me?"*

* *Find a sponsor: somebody who can give your idea powerful support in the organization.*

* *Identify the people who will help to implement the idea. How will they need to change their*

behaviour? How soon can you involve them? How will you motivate them to do what you want them to do?

* *Set milestones for yourself. They will help to motivate you. Reaching each milestone is a sign of progress and an opportunity to pat yourself on the back.*

Force field analysis

Ultimately, an idea will only be successfully implemented when people change their behaviour.

In an organization, more people will be involved in implementing a new idea than in formulating it: more people will own the solution than owned the problem. If we are to influence their behaviour, we have to understand the complex sets of forces within which they operate. We must take a systems approach.

Any human system —a company, a family, a school, a team —can be thought of as being in a state of dynamic equilibrium. A number of forces operate on it in different directions, and the balance of these forces makes the system stable. Without this balance the energies within the system would tear it apart.

Implementing a new idea will change the balance of forces and threaten the system's stability. It is for this reason that human systems resist change. Pushing in a given direction will create equal and opposite pressure; pushing harder will only increase resistance. The system will only move in a desired direction if we *decrease* or *remove* the forces resisting change.

Force field analysis creates a simple, clear model of the forces promoting and resisting change in a given direction.

FORCE FIELD ANALYSIS

Present situation ⟶ *Desired situation*

Personal
Interpersonal
Group/team/department
Intergroup/team/department
Organizational
Administrative
Technological
Environmental

Driving forces ⟶ ⟵ *Restraining forces*

(needs, dissatisfactions,   *(Economic costs,*
shared visions)   *psychological costs)*

When conducting a force field analysis, take care to:

* confine the analysis to a specific, local group of people — a single team, department or managerial group;

* analyse the forces at work on that group —not on individuals within the group or on the people conducting the analysis;

* consider only the forces you know to be at work — not possible, likely or hypothetical forces.

Pursue your analysis in a systematic way.

1. Define the change you want as specifically as possible, as it affects the group under consideration ("how to . . .).

2. As driving forces for change, look particularly for:

    * needs within the group;
    * shared dissatisfactions;
    * a shared vision of success.

3.   As restraining forces, consider:

*   financial costs (which may not be easily
       quantifiable);
*   psychological costs (the resistances that may
       result from change rather than what may
       already exist).

Address each of these restraining forces using 'how
to's'.

4.   It will now be possible to begin developing an
     implementation plan. Actions, both long-term and
     immediate, can be mapped out — tentatively and
     provisionally.

General questions to ask in drawing up the action plan
will probably include the following.

*   What is the relative importance of the forces
      indicated in our analysis?
*   To which people and forces do we have immediate
      access?
*   Where do we have influence?
*   What is the state of readiness for change within the
      group?
*   How can we deal with the psychological costs of
      change sensitively?
*   Where will the vital links between
      people have to be forged to create change?
*   What are the consequences of failing to change?

WHICH IMPLEMENTATION PLAN?

Long term	Short term
Low control	*High control*
Long timescale	*Short timescale*
Authority of others needed	*No further*
Large numbers of	*authorization needed*
people involved	*Few people involved*

Implementation may set off a whole new set of creative explorations, beginning with questions like:

* how to involve those likely to be affected by change;
* how to let people know what's going on;
* how to minimize fears of the unknown;
* how to demonstrate the benefits of change to those affected;
* how to test the idea on a small scale.

SELLING IDEAS: a checklist

* *How will this idea serve the mission or objectives of my organization?*
* *What assets do I have to champion this idea?*
* *What resources do I have to promote the idea?*
* *What do I need to promote the idea?*
* *Who will be affected if the idea is implemented?*
* *Who can become my ally?*
* *Why should they support me?*
* *Who could I add to my band of supporters?*
* *How do I convince them?*
* *Who can I trust for reliable feedback?*
* *Who will be my opponents?*
* *What resources do my opponents have to oppose me?*
* *What resistance can I anticipate?*
* *How can I minimize its impact?*
* *Who are our competitors in this area?*
* *What are they doing?*
* *What aspects of my idea am I willing to alter or sacrifice?*
* *How could I test or pilot this idea with minimum risk?*
* *Why do I like this idea so much?*

---

9 creative conversations

The most important work in the new economy is creating conversations.   [Alan Webber]

An organization is a network of conversations. The quality of its work depends increasingly on the quality of the conservations that take place in and around it.

Creativity has a vital role to play in developing our conversational skills. The way we think affects the way we converse. And, by the same token, the nature of our conservations influences our mental patterns.

Debate, discussion, or dialogue?

Conversation, they say, is a lost art. Very few people are trained to converse (from the Latin, originally meaning 'to move around with'). Our education mostly stresses the importance of *arguing*: of taking a position, holding it, maintaining it, convincing others of its worth, and destroying any position that threatens it.

The polite name for this activity is **debate** (from the Latin, 'to beat down'). Ideas are pitted against one another in a verbal boxing match, and the idea left standing at the end is considered to be 'correct'.

Debate (in more or less polite forms) uses second-stage thinking to fuel verbal conflict. Ideas are presented, sponsored, challenged, supported, opposed, attacked, outflanked, defeated — but rarely *examined*.

Certainties become more entrenched; assumptions are left unquestioned; ambiguities are ignored.

The adversarial nature of debate means that ideas come to be identified with the people advocating them. To attack an idea is to attack its sponsor; to support it is to create an alliance. We begin to use conversational gambits, ploys, manoeuvres and defence mechanisms, not to develop the conversation but to play politics.

Identifying ideas with individuals also leads to a dangerous confusion between rational and emotional responses. Enormous energy can be devoted to *preventing* emotions from overwhelming debate; but the dynamic of debate means that the polarisation of emotions is an inevitable element of the process.

Discussion is a more useful form of conversation using second-stage thinking. In discussion (from the Latin, 'to shake apart'), we dissect and analyse a subject of common concern. We have a purpose in mind: to reach a decision, to achieve agreement, to find common ground, to identify priorities, to organize a plan of action.

Discussion has a clear *focus*: to get something done. By clarifying our objective, we can prevent a discussion from collapsing into sterile debate.

The purpose of **dialogue** is to find something new: the meanings that we can create between us. In dialogue (from the Greek, 'meaning flowing through'), we are exploring each other's understanding, and offering our own for examination. We try to find the assumptions underlying our ideas in order to transform our understanding of them, and to realize the potential that lies in them. Our goal is not to find the 'common ground' of consensus or negotiation, but to construct a new, shared meaning.

> I 'win' or 'lose' a debate. In dialogue the other is my partner or fellow explorer in a mutually creative enterprise of discovery.
>
> [Danah Zohar]

A creative conversation will include elements of both dialogue and discussion: dialogue to encourage first-stage thinking, developing our perceptions and exploring possibilities; discussion to facilitate second-stage thinking, when we are 'shaking ideas apart', evaluating them and developing them into workable plans of action.

It is important to be clear where you are at any point in such a conversation. What are you attempting to achieve? Focus clearly on the *goal* of the conversation and where you are starting from: shared and differing intentions, agreed areas of concern, suggested means of pursuing your objectives.

TELLING AND ASKING

Dialogue and discussion both create a dynamic between telling and asking.

Debate, of course, does not involve questions at all. Most managers (to hazard a dangerous generalization) have been well drilled in the techniques of assertion: in presenting a case, arguing for it and explaining it. We are often less skilled at asking: investigating an issue, exploring it, examining the assumptions or values that lie behind it.

This imbalance is reinforced by organizational cultures that value certainty, decisiveness and the ability to stand your ground. Assertiveness (or aggressiveness) is generally rewarded; uncertainty and doubt tend to be regarded as signs of weakness.

> *Questioning is not the mode of conservation among gentlemen.*
>
> [Samuel Johnson]

These broad tendencies are changing: partly because 'macho' styles of management are themselves being challenged. Managers increasingly recognize the need to balance these two modes of conversation: to balance, in Peter Senge's terms, advocacy with inquiry.

The ladder of inference

Chris Argyris has formulated a powerful model for understanding and influencing the course of conservations.

Argyris pictures mental processing as a ladder. At the bottom of the ladder is observation; at the top, action.

*   From our **observation**, we step onto the first rung of the ladder by selecting data.

*   On the second rung, we add **meaning** from our experience of similar data.

*   On the third, we make **assumptions** that generalize those meanings.

*   On the fourth, we construct mental patterns (**beliefs** or 'theories') out of those assumptions.

The mental patterns dictate our actions.

We travel up and down this mental ladder all the time. So skilled are we at climbing it, that we can actually leap all the rungs in a matter of seconds. Such 'leaps of abstraction' substitute generalizations for observation of reality and treat these generalizations as 'facts'.

Our mental patterns can help us to leap *down* the ladder by dictating what data to select in future (what William Isaacs has called 'a reflexive loop'). This is a mindset in operation.

USING THE LADDER OF INFERENCE

We can use the ladder to:

*   make our thinking more visible to others;

*   ask others about their thinking;

*   offer our own thinking for examination, by ourselves and others.

THE LADDER OF INFERENCE

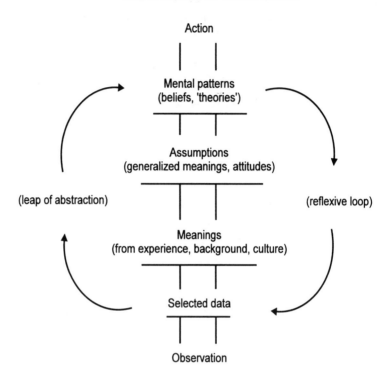

Action

Mental patterns
(beliefs, 'theories')

Assumptions
(generalized meanings, attitudes)

(leap of abstraction)   (reflexive loop)

Meanings
(from experience, background, culture)

Selected data

Observation

This last is an important attitude to adopt, if we are to engage in a genuine search for common meaning. Others may initially be surprised at our willingness to renounce ownership of our ideas. Once our intentions are clear, however, the effect on the overall dynamic of the conversation can be dramatic.

Simply by *pausing* on the ladder and looking about us, we can find new perceptions, and alternative interpretations.

Once we have paused, we can *choose* to move up or down the ladder together.

We can step down from a stated assumption to the meanings that gave rise to it, and the data that we used in the first place. Once at the base of the ladder with data, we can decide whether this ladder is the only ladder we can climb, or whether the data suggests other possible meanings, other assumptions, theories and possible courses of action.

Or we might slowly walk up the ladder, asking what meanings are suggested by an important piece of data, what we are able to infer from it, and how we might generalize from it to form the rationale for a course of action.

Use these interventions whenever you have the opportunity. They do not require any special training or awareness on the part of anybody else. And they can have an immediate, dramatic effect on the quality of your conversations.

MAKING OUR THINKING MORE VISIBLE TO OTHERS

Action	*"This is what I think we should do."*
Mental patterns	*"I think that, in general . . ." (beliefs, 'theories')*
Assumptions (generalized meanings, attitudes)	*"I've made this assumption, because . . ."*
Meanings (from experience, background, culture)	*"Let me give you an example."*
Selected data	*"This is what I've been looking at."*
Observation	

ASKING OTHERS ABOUT THEIR THINKING

Action	*"What leads you to suggest this?"* *(avoid "Why?")* *"What makes this a good plan?"*
Mental patterns *(beliefs, 'theories')*	*"Can you take me through your thinking?"* *"How does this relate to that?"* *"I'm lost on this stage."*
Assumptions *(generalized* *meanings,* *attitudes)*	*"I wonder whether you're assuming . . .?"* *This seems to contradict . . ."* *"Have you considered . . ."* *"When you say that, I wonder whether it* *means that . . .?"*
Meanings *(from experience,* *background,* *culture)*	*"How would this affect . . .?"* *"Am I correct you're saying . . .?*
Selected data	*"What led you to look at this in particular?"* *"Have you looked at . . .?*
Observation	

OFFERING OUR THINKING FOR EXAMINATION

Action	*"Can you see any flaws in my reasoning?"*
Mental patterns (beliefs, 'theories')	*"Would you organize this stuff differently?"*
	"Do you see things differently?"
Assumptions (generalized meanings, attitudes)	*"Are my assumptions valid?"*
	"In what circumstances?"
Meanings (from experience, background, culture)	*"You must remember I see it like this because . . ."*
	"Do you interpret it in some other way?"
Selected data	*"Is my observation correct?"*
	"Have I missed anything?"
Observation	

Creative listening

Any conversation includes listening. Creative listening, though, is more than just hearing what someone is saying to us. We must also stop ourselves walking up (or down) our own ladders of inference instead of listening. It is all too easy to start:

* judging (adding our own meanings, creating assumptions, confirming beliefs);
* feeling superior;
* comparing;
* rehearsing what we're going to say next;
* thinking about something else;
* trying to listen to something else.

> *Respect for others begins with not ignoring their words.*
>
> [Elias Canetti]

We can use listening as an opportunity to use our intuition; to relax our own thinking; and to look for clues that could take the conservation in fruitful and unexpected directions.

THE TEN COMMANDMENTS OF CREATIVE LISTENING

1. **Stop talking.**

   To others; and to yourself! You cannot listen if you are talking.

2. **Demonstrate your interest.**

   Take notes or draw pattern diagrams. But no doodling, shuffling, fiddling or looking about.

3. **Don't interrupt.**

   Let pauses happen past your tolerance level. Try not to finish sentences for the speaker.

4. **Put yourself in the speaker's shoes.**

   Imagine yourself in their position, doing their work, facing their difficulties. Imagine how they might regard you.

5. **Listen to what your intuition may be trying to tell you.**

   About body language, tone of voice, eye contact. Be careful.

6. **Listen for 'creative triggers'.**

   Note down metaphors, analogies, figures of speech, evocative or emotive words that might prove interesting starting points for excursions.

---

7. **Encourage.**

Show that you are keen that the speaker should continue. Go easy on critical or judgemental comments.

8. **Check your understanding.**

Repeat what the speaker has just told you at an appropriate point. Try to rephrase but use the speaker's language.

9. **Ask: "what's good about it?"**

Which point can you add to, build on, develop? Cultivate "yes and" rather than "yes but".

10. **Stop talking.**

This is first and last: all the other commandments depend on it.

Shhhh!!

10 coaching for creativity

Think wrongly if you please, but in all cases think for yourself.
[Doris Lessing]

One of our most important roles as managers is to help release the potential of those we manage.

Responsibility, motivation, involvement: these qualities we would all want to foster. Most of us recognize that *telling* people to take responsibility, to motivate themselves or to become more involved is self-defeating. Carrots and sticks may be useful short-term, or in a crisis, but they are minimally effective as motivators.

In the end, people can only motivate themselves to develop. Coaching, at its best, is designed to help them do that.

> *Coaching is unlocking a person's potential to maximize their own performance. It is helping them to learn rather than teaching them.*
> [John Whitmore]

This is essentially a creative endeavour. Coaches seek to transform the perceptions of the people being coached so that they, in turn, can transform their own approach to their work. Whether we are managing individuals or a team, creative coaching can help to bring that double transformation about.

Creativity and confidence

We are all naturally creative. Given the right circumstances, we will explore and manipulate our environment in imaginative ways. These circumstances include:

* clear guidelines and objectives
* being supported through difficulties
* feeling a sense of belonging
* praise and encouragement

These elements contribute to a sense of psychological security: the confidence that is essential if we are to be creative.

Confidence ⟶ Creativity

When we are confident, we become more playful —— and I'm entirely sure that playfulness and creativity are indistinguishable — [John Cleese]

Many factors at work can threaten this sense of confidence:

* an increased emphasis on accountability
* externally imposed goals, targets and performance measures
* increased workloads
* organizational change
* altered conditions of employment
* performance-related pay or reward schemes

All these can *diminish* our willingness to take responsibility, motivate ourselves to give more or use our initiative.

Creative coaching can be highly effective in countering these debilitating factors. Indeed, it can actually help to *increase* our sense of psychological security by equipping us to handle life's uncertainties more effectively.

Coaching can create a reinforcing cycle, creativity and confidence continually amplifying each other.

The fundamentals of coaching

Coaching is about helping somebody to improve their own performance. At the heart of the coaching relationship is a partnership. An effective coach helps coachees to think for themselves, fostering greater **awareness** and **responsibility**.

KEY AIMS OF COACHING

To build AWARENESS	*— of what is going on*
	— of goals
	— of what we need to know
(1st stage thinking: perception)	*— of dynamics, relationships, and wider organizational issues*
	— of options for action
	— and inner awareness: of fears, emotions, desires, intuitions, capabilities
To encourage RESPONSIBILITY	*— for ideas*
	— for decisions
(2nd stage thinking: judgement)	*— for future action*

The essence of the coach's role is to ask questions. *This point cannot be stressed too heavily*. Instructing will tend to generate a minimal response: the action carried out, but little more. Asking a question focuses attention, increases awareness and encourages the coachee to take responsibility.

> *What I hear I forget*
> *What I see I remember*
> *What I do I know* [Chinese proverb]

Asking questions also helps the coach. Instead of forging ahead with a sequence of orders, the coach can use questions to follow the coachee's trains of thought, their interest or enthusiasm, their emotional reactions — — and adapt the coaching accordingly.

Of course, it is essential for the coach to *listen* to the coachee's answers — and pick up on them. Coaching should be a genuine dialogue (see Chapter 9, 'Creative Conversations').

The most effective questions are those that encourage the coachee to think for themselves. The coach's task is not to transfer expertise, nor to emphasize the coachee's accountability. Questions that point up the coachee's ignorance or subservience are unhelpful.

The coach, then, should be careful to ask *genuine* questions: not rhetorical, sarcastic, facetious, loaded or leading questions. Ask questions that:

* indicate how well the coach understands a situation;
* suggest what to ask next;
* monitor the coachee's progress against an objective;
* promote responsibility in the coachee for a decision.

The best kinds of questions are open, non-judgemental and specific.

During first-stage thinking, when we are fostering clearer awareness, the coach should ask questions that require quantifiable answers:

* "What? Where? When? Who? How many? How much?"

Avoid "Why?" and "How?". They will inevitably imply judgement, analysis or criticism: all of them forms of second-stage thinking. If necessary, "Why?" can become "What were the reasons for . . .?" and "How?" might be better put as "What were the steps that . . .?"

During second-stage thinking, the same kinds of questions can serve to focus on what the coachee will do next, how, when, where and so on.

The Ladder of Inference (chapter 9) is a useful tool in this process. Walking the coachee down the ladder from beliefs or assumptions to specific observations will encourage a wider awareness; walking up the ladder through meanings, judgement and belief to action will strengthen motivation and a sense of responsibility for future actions.

CAN A MANAGER BE A COACH?

Is it possible for a line manager to fill the role of coach? How can we square the admirable aims of creative coaching with our other managerial roles?

The critical issue here is *accountability*. It may be difficult to engage in a genuine dialogue when the coachee is accountable to you for performance standards or meeting targets. Unless accountability is clearly recognized and acknowledged, it can become a demon overshadowing the entire coaching process.

On the other hand, the line manager may be in the best possible position to act as coach: they may know the coachee better than anybody else in the organization. And they are is best placed to deal with these very issues of accountability.

The best policy must be to clarify as exactly aspossible the standards, targets and key responsibilities for which the coachee is accountable to you. Indeed, coaching can provide an opportunity for the coachee to become more aware of the reasons for them and therefore more responsible for meeting them.

Inevitably, coaching is a delicate and sensitive process. It requires the very best qualities of any manager:

*keen listening and observation   *integrity
*detachment   *supportiveness
*interest   *patience

A good coach must be able to empathize with the coachee and yet retain a keen sense of self-awareness. Intuition and the ability to withhold judgement are vital.

At its most creative, the coaching process actually challenges our own observation, values, assumptions, and beliefs as managers. Coaching can be a good opportunity to re-examine our own awareness and sense of responsibility. It can become a dialogue which results in learning on both sides: a genuine partnership. Coaching can be the most rewarding part of our role as a manager.

CREATIVE COACHING

There are four parts to the coaching process:

*   GOAL setting: for the session and for the coachee's development;

*   REALITY analysis, to explore the current situation for difficulties and opportunities;

*   OPTIONS for future courses of action;

*   WHAT to do: a 'hard' decision on action, WHEN and by WHOM.

In each part, first-stage thinking helps to foster *awareness* of current reality and potential; and second-stage thinking encourages the coachee to take *responsibility* for a course of action.

Goal setting

The initial task is to decide the purpose of the coaching: to establish our goal, both for the coaching session itself and for the performance issue being coached.

First-stage thinking here is a matter of reviewing and proliferating goals. A goal is a **constructed problem** (chapter 5): and the most useful tool to use in formulating it is '**How to**' (chapter 5). Use '**Backwards planning**' (also chapter 5) to explore the coachee's deeper values, his or her higher aspirations and longer-term ambitions.

Using these tools will generate a large number of possible goals. Some will be, in Whitmore's terms, 'end goals'; others will be 'performance goals', measurable levels of performance that may set you on the path to an end goal or prove that you've achieved it. All of them are revealing: but only one or two can be chosen for immediate coaching.

Second-stage thinking now comes into play. The best goals to choose, for practical purposes, are those that generate the greatest **creative tension** between goal and reality. Like the tension in a taut elastic band that stores potential energy, it is creative tension that will provide the energy for movement.

The goal should be *attainable* —not beyond the coachee's capabilities or out of his or her reach; but also *challenging* enough to maintain the tension.

Above all, it is the *coachee* who should make the choice of goal. The coach's role is to help the coachee decide how attainable and challenging the goal is, and review it in the wider context of the coachee's work responsibilities and objectives.

Reality checking

Creative tension depends as much on a clear perception of reality, of course, as on a clear goal.

Use first-stage thinking to look reality coolly in the face. Be objective; avoid judgement. Instead of describing past performance, for example, as 'bad' or 'inadequate', focus on the specific aspects of it that need improvement. Walk the coachee down the Ladder of Inference and offer verifiable, measurable observations.

> "What have you tried so far?"
> "What were the results?"
> "Exactly how much under target did you come in?"
> "What resources do you lack?"
> "When did you last check the situation?"
> "Where were the actual difficulties?"

Remember that a good deal of current reality is *inner reality*. Follow where the coachee's concerns take you and (gently) investigate their emotional responses.

> "How did you feel when you tried . . .?"
> "What emotions arise when you talk about . . .?"
> "Is there anything you're afraid of?"
> "How do you think you might be preventing yourself from achieving more?"
> "How confident do you feel right now about achieving this goal?"

Robert Fritz claims that virtually all of us have been programmed from a very early age with two deep-seated beliefs that inhibit our ability to pursue challenging goals:

* a sense of **powerlessness**: that we are incapable of achieving what we want;

* a sense of **unworthiness**: that, in some way, we don't deserve to succeed.

These beliefs — and there are few of us who have not experienced one or other of them — are part of current reality. Surfacing them can help both coach and coachee to understand the deeper reasons for reluctance, hostility or concern about pursuing a goal. Facing our demons can help us to conquer them.

It is as well, however, to be cautious in this area: you are coaching, not counselling. If in doubt: leave alone.

Use second-stage thinking to assess which aspects of reality are most relevant to your goals.

Options for action

This is potentially the most creative part of the coaching process. Our purpose here is to find as many options for action as possible, in order to choose specific, realistic 'next steps'.

First-stage thinking here will use every creative tool and technique at our disposal to explore the available options — and those that seem not to be available!

* pattern diagrams
* rule reversal
* discovering assumptions
* intermediate impossibles
* metaphorical thinking
* virtual worlds
* consulting an oracle

Once again, it is important to recognize that inner reality may be inhibiting the choice. *"The opponent within one's own head"*, to use Timothy Gallwey's phrase, can be a powerful censor.

"It can't be done."
"We can't do it like that."
"They would never agree to it."
"It will be too expensive."
"Altogether too risky/disruptive/complicated/radical . . ."
"I don't have the time."
"That's already been tried — and look what
    happened."

The coach can counter these objections with *"What if . . .?"* questions:

> "What if we could do it?"
> "What if we could get them to agree?"
> "What if we found a budget?"
> "What if we managed the risk/minimized disruption/ made it simpler . . .?"
> "What if we reallocated resources?"
> "What if we tried again?"

Choosing an option is very much a second-stage thinking task. Carefully examine the costs and benefits of the action; list its positive, negative and interesting aspects. Don't limit yourselves to one option: it may be possible to merge two or more as a realistic course of action, or schedule options as immediate and longer-term.

Check that the chosen option is:

*attainable   — budgeted, costed, properly resourced
              — specific and measurable
              — realistic in wider organizational terms
              — scheduled

*challenging   — requires new activity or research
              — excites the coachee
              — moves reality closer to the goal (and doesn't lower the goal!)
              — enhances or adds skills
              — will improve performance
              — will be a genuine learning experience

What to do

This part of the coaching process is about drawing up a detailed action plan:

> "What are you going to do?"
> "When will you do it?"
> "Will this action (or series of actions) move you towards your goal?"

"What barriers might you have to overcome?"
"Who else will be involved?"
"What support do you need? Where will you find it?"
"What other consequences are there of this course
of action, and how do we deal with them?"

First-stage thinking will offer questions such as:

"What else could you do?"
"Could you do it differently?"
"Are there other ways of meeting this target or
goal?"
"What if this barrier didn't exist?"

And it is vital for the coach to ask:

"What can I do to help?"

But this part of coaching requires a lot of hard-headed second-stage thinking if an action plan is going to be workable — and if the coachee is actually going to carry it through.

It is critically important, too, to establish issues of accountability, if only to clear them out of the way. How will the coachee be accountable to you in this plan? What targets shall we set? Might we need to review them? If so, when? Ideally, these accountable targets should be *minimal* and *agreed* between coach and coachee — as they would at an appraisal.

It is a good ideal to document the agreed action plan, and even sign it, to confirm that the coachee is committed to carrying it through. Build in a review date to monitor progress.

Creativity and teamwork

Teams provide a golden opportunity to develop creativity. A good team environment can provide excellent pre-conditions for creative thinking; and groups of people can produce more interesting ideas, and in greater numbers, than an individual.

Creativity, in turn, can bring enormous benefits to the team. By helping it to find new ideas and challenging assumptions, creativity can help to strengthen a team, renew its values and redefine its identity.

> *None of us are as smart as all of us.*
> [Japanese proverb]

Every team is composed of individuals. It depends on the diverse talents of its members. Too strong an emphasis on team spirit can actually stifle creativity. The result will be 'groupthink', in which mindsets are reinforced, behaviours become automatic and performance suffers.

Once again, the benefits of teamwork and creativity are mutual. A healthy team will encourage individuals to think flexibly, express their thoughts freely, suggest,

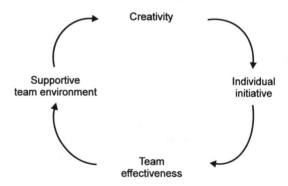

question and challenge. And creative thinking will help to develop precisely the team environment in which those things can happen. A creative team will find itself in a cycle of positive, reinforcing behaviour, continually reinventing, re-energizing and re-aligning itself.

PRECONDITIONS FOR CREATIVE TEAMWORK

Where should we intervene to start creative coaching with a team?

Setting up creativity sessions 'cold' may do more harm than good. People need to feel secure that they are not being forced into unknown territory against their will. They need to recognize the goals of such sessions, and to understand clearly the tools they will use during them.

Prior even to this, pay attention to the broader preconditions that will allow creativity to develop more easily in the team.

* **Develop and train the team.**

Team members need to know one another's strengths and approaches to working. They also need to be trained in the tools and techniques of creativity.

* **Involve all the team in establishing the team's vision, mission, objectives, tasks and values.**

* **Individuals should have clear action responsibilities.**

Job descriptions should include the unique and essential elements of every team member's job. This will help to give people ownership of work, and of any problems they may bring to the creativity session.

* **Wherever possible, give individuals *complete* tasks.**

Ownership of the whole of a piece of work — responsibility for it and control over it — will help to encourage a more creative approach to it, as well as promoting motivation, satisfaction and general mental well-being.

* **Seize every opportunity to offer challenging tasks.**

People are much more likely to want to be creative if their work provides opportunities to develop their skills and knowledge.

* **Have clear procedures for team involvement in individual tasks.**

People should feel comfortable asking — and being asked — for help. Creativity is easily stifled by feelings of resentment or possessiveness.

* **Try to maximize the authority of the team and minimize control by external authority.**

Often a difficult task. The team leader — or manager — has a particular responsibility for acting as an effective interface between the team and the organization. This may require creativity in itself!

* **Encourage creative conversations and lead by example.**

Take every opportunity to lead by doing, rather than telling. Demonstrate that expressing doubt or ambiguity are acceptable. Examine assumptions and mental patterns without criticizing them. Use the Ladder of Inference, particularly to welcome enquiry into your own thinking.

* **Make creative activity a planned part of the team's work.**

Set up creativity sessions, where the tools and techniques of creative thinking can be practised, and where team members can present problems for creative treatment.

Running a creativity session

This straightforward programme relies on a few essential principles.

1. It must be led.

2. The process is structured in stages; each stage must be completed before moving on to the next.

3. The whole team takes part (or up to about eight people if the team is larger).

4. There is a 'client' who brings a problem to the session. It is important that one person should 'own' both the initial problem and the solution. Like any client, they should be treated with the greatest respect!

The client may be a team member, or — once the team gains a reputation as an internal 'creative consultancy' — may come from outside. Before the session begins, clients should be clear that:

*they truly own the problem;
*they honestly want to solve it;
*they are in a position to do something about it;
*they don't already know the answer;
*they are genuinely open to new suggestions.

Leader's notes

The session leader's primary task is to create a climate in which the team feel secure. Like any coach, you are a facilitator of the process: you must provide the conditions in which people can perform, not provide answers.

*   Make the rules clear at the beginning and help the team to keep to the structure.

*   Encourage concentration by the way you arrange the furniture. Issue notepads so that people can record their own ideas rapidly.

*   Make sure that everybody's contribution is recorded, acknowledged and valued.

*   Discourage judgement, confrontational questions or evaluative remarks during idea generation. Do not simply reject them; ask how they can be converted into speculative suggestions or restatements of the problem ("how to").

* Do not offer your own ideas. Your authority as leader will lend them a weight that may be inappropriate. Similarly, don't evaluate, edit, censor or restate other people's ideas.

* If the team gets stuck, refer them to the process so that they can restart themselves.

* If you must intervene, do so in a non-manipulative way. Repeat one of the team's earlier ideas; throw in a 'bunch of bananas' (or some other totally unrelated image or metaphor); or suggest a break.

* Praise the group, not individuals.

* Be sensitive to group dynamics. Encourage quiet team members and try to avoid allowing dominant members to hijack a session — perhaps by ruling that all ideas should be written down in silence, and collected as a separate activity.

* Encourage creative listening.

* Set targets: numbers of ideas, time limits. Make it clear, however, that targets are minimal: the group should keep going if they achieve their quota of ideas in the given time.

Warm-up session

As in any other form of training, a warm-up session is vital to loosen up, relax and get the 'creativity muscles' working.

It is important to emphasize playfulness. Put the team into the right frame of mind by taking two or three creativity tools and playing with them.

Warm-up games might include:

* word association around a single word;
* using the oracle (a good dictionary) to bisociate pairs of words chosen at random (use dice for rapid generation of numbers);

* rule reversal on proverbs;
* discovering assumptions behind a mission statement, quality procedure or 'buzz word' by associating, pattern planning and analogy;
* uses/non-uses of any household object to create intermediate impossibles, leading to concept challenge;
* taking a 'how to' task and developing it by a metaphorical excursion or a trip to a 'virtual world'.

Problem stage

The team's goal at this stage is to take the client's 'How to' statement and generate as many new "how to" statements as possible from it.

* The client describes the task (use the 'Task Description' checklist in chapter 5), using as much concrete, evocative language as possible.

* The team listen to the description, noting down 'trigger' words and any words provoked in their own minds by words in the description.

* Individuals then translate each 'trigger' word into a new "how to" statement, writing each on a separate Post-It note.

* All the Post-Its are put on the wall and categorized as **realistic, embryonic** and **implausible**.

* The client is invited to choose one or two of the new 'how to's' to carry over to the next stage. Concentrate on the **implausible** category and try to find the most evocative, mysterious, or exciting 'how to'.

Idea stage

Split the team into groups of three or four.

The groups' goal, at this stage, is to bring back to the client _three_ ideas for tackling the problem.

Explain that solutions should be realistic, but not necessarily feasible. They need not be worked out in detail: a single sentence supported by a brief explanation is all that we need.

Set a time limit (probably about 30 minutes).

It may be important not to involve the client at this stage, to stop him or her influencing a group's thinking with critical or negative comments.

Each group now takes the new 'How to' and applies whatever tools and techniques they wish.

*   Take a single word and, individually, create a body of word associations from it. Gather the group's lists together and pick the most colourful or 'unlikely' words.

*   You could use these to search for possible assumptions lying behind the 'how to'.

*   You could 'force-fit' some of them back to the original word in the "how to" statement and find the bisociation. Use this bisociation to find a possible solution.

*   You could bisociate two of the words on your list and then 'force-fit' your bisociation back to the 'how to' statement, generating a possible solution.

*   You could use one of the generated words as the start of a metaphorical excursion. Explore the 'virtual world' you have entered and ask how the problem would be solved there. Bring back those solutions, transformed into realistic solutions.

At the end of this stage, each group makes a brief presentation to the client of the three solutions they propose.

The client is invited to choose the solution they find most attractive.

Solution stage

The goal at this stage is to develop the chosen solution into a feasible proposal.

* The client paraphrases the chosen idea back to the group to demonstrate that they understand it. Be careful to describe it, not to make judgements about it.

* Client and team together identify **positive**, **negative** and **interesting** aspects of the idea, transforming negatives into ideas for further development.

* Finally run the *NAF* check. Is the proposal novel, attractive and feasible?

* Decide the next steps. What are we going to do with this proposal?

PROGRAMME FOR A CREATIVITY SESSION

*Warm-up session
(creativity exercises: unrelated to the
'main problem')*

PROBLEM STAGE

*Problems as stated:
'How to'*

Description by client

*Team use 'trigger' words to generate
new 'How to's'*

*New 'How to's' are categorized:
realistic, embryonic, implausible*

*Client chooses a new 'How to':
problem as understood*

IDEA STAGE

Team splits into smaller groups

*Many ideas are generated for tackling the problem:
creative techniques*

Promising ideas are presented to the client

Client chooses a solution

SOLUTION STAGE

Client paraphrases solution

*Team and client list positive, negative and
interesting aspects of the
solution*

Solution checked: new, attractive, feasible?

Next steps: formulation of action plan

further reading

Buzan, Tony: *The Mind Map Book*, BBC, 1993, — *Use Your Head*, BBC, 1974.

de Bono, Edward: *Lateral Thinking for Management*, Penguin, 1982. — *Teach Your Child to Think*, Penguin, 1993.

Fritz, Robert: T*he Path of Least Resistance*. Fawcett-Columbine, 1989. — *Creating*. Fawcett-Columbine, 1991.

Goldberg, Phillip: *The Intuitive Edge*. Tarcher, 1983.

Henry, Jane (ed.): *Creative Management*. Open University, 1991.

Koestler, Arthur: *The Act of Creation*. Picador, 1975.

Majaro, Simon: *Managing Ideas for Profit*. McGraw-Hill, 1992.

Nolan, Vincent: *The Innovator's Handbook*, Sphere, 1989.

Prince, George M: The Practice of Creativity. Harper and Row, 1970.

Rickards, Tudor: Creativity and Problem-solving at Work, Gower, 1990.

Senge, Peter: *The Fifth Discipline*. Century Business, 1992.

Senge, Peter et al: *The Fifth Discipline Fieldbook*, Brealey, 1994.

von Oech, Roger: *A Whack on the Side of the Head*. Thorsons, 1990.

Wheatley, M J: *Leadership and the New Science*, Berrett-Koehler, 1992.

Whitmore, John: *Coaching for Performance*. Brealey, 1992.

Zohar, Danah: *The Quantum Self*, Flamingo, 1991.

Zohar, Danah and Marshall, Ian: *The Quantum Society*, Flamingo, 1994.